BIRDFEEDER
HANDBOOK

The Royal Society for the Protection of Birds

BIRDFEEDER HANDBOOK

ROBERT BURTON

PHOTOGRAPHY
KIM TAYLOR

DEALERFIELD

A Dorling Kindersley Book

Art Editor Caroline Murray
Project Editor Roger Smoothy

First published in Great Britain in 1990
by Dorling Kindersley Limited,
9 Henrietta Street, London WC2E 8PS

Third impression 1991
Fourth impression 1993

British Library Cataloguing in Publication Data
Burton, Robert, *1941–*
  RSPB Birdfeeder Handbook.
  1. Great Britain. Gardens. Birds. Care
  I. Title II. Royal Society for the Protection of Birds
  639.9′782941

  ISBN 0-907305-61-X
          Colour separation by
Fotographics Limited, London – Hong Kong

          Printed and bound in Italy
          by New Interlitho, Milan

CONTENTS

CHAPTER ONE

THE BIRD GARDEN

As THE COUNTRYSIDE changes and more land is made available to house an ever-growing human population, gardens have become increasingly important as bird habitats. This chapter presents a bird's-eye view of the garden. It covers the broad range of birds that are likely to visit, what features they find attractive in a garden and how you can improve your garden to tempt more birds to spend time there. Success in attracting birds is less a matter of observing strict rules, which may conflict with your interests as a gardener, than following guidelines to make the most of possibilities that already exist. Even if you live in a built-up area without access to a garden, there are plenty of other chances to observe birds. Fortunately, most towns and cities have pockets of open spaces that support a surprising amount of wildlife.

An overgrown garden – an excellent bird habitat

∴ WATCHING GARDEN BIRDS ∴

E VEN THE SMALLEST OF urban gardens attracts a variety of birds that is equally as interesting as the more spectacular and less familiar species that live in remote, wild locations. Although you can enjoy simply sharing your garden with birds, if you take some time to watch what they are doing, there is a wealth of discoveries to be made in the unlikeliest of places.

• PLENTY TO SEE •

Across the lawn from my window there is a bird-table with a dangling peanut bag, tit-bell and scrap basket, where a menu of seeds, fat and kitchen leftovers is offered to the neighbourhood's birds. The birds fly in and out across a backdrop of cypresses, quick-growing trees popular for hedging and screening. I have never liked these dark, impenetrable conifers, thinking them sterile and dull and, when allowed to grow beyond the height strictly necessary for privacy, a definite eyesore. Why, I often wonder, do more people not take a longer view and plant something interesting like hawthorn, beech or fast-growing willow?

I have had to change my mind about my neighbour's cypress trees. The more I watch the comings and goings of the birds in my garden, the more I find that the cypresses are full of activity. The birds do not

The bird-table
Equipped with peanut bags and other hanging feeders, a bird-table will lure birds into your garden. Place one close to a large window so that you can see the visiting birds clearly.

share my prejudices: blue tits search for insects on the branchlets of soft leaves, while shy dunnocks and wrens forage on the bare ground under the trees, and I am certain that several birds creep among the foliage to roost at night. A dusty and aromatic foray into the dark recesses revealed the old, disused nest of a goldcrest and there is a robin nesting in a hollow as I write. The most interesting discovery has been that greenfinches clamber along the branches at the top of the trees and peck at the marble-sized cones. I can see them chewing the seed scales as their stout beaks are silhouetted against the clear morning sky. My bird books make no mention of greenfinches attacking the cones of

Eye-opener *Seeing greenfinches coming to feed on cypress cones is a delightful surprise.*

cypresses or any other conifer, but I have since learnt that, although a greenfinch's bill is too broad to probe into cones, it can wrench the seeds out of any that are already open. There are always things to learn about birdlife and a chance to experience an exciting thrill of discovery when observing something new.

I have set the scene for this book with an account of the birdlife in my cypress trees to show that even a simple garden, containing the dullest screening trees or surrounding hedges, attracts a variety of birds. Eighteen species of bird regularly make use of my garden in winter and another half-dozen occasionals add some excitement. I am lucky to be surrounded by farmland but, for all its rural surroundings, this is an ordinary garden. Plants have been chosen by previous owners for show rather than as bait to attract birds and there is no room for the miniature wilderness of wild plants so often regarded as essential for a wildlife garden.

Life among the cypresses There is plenty to discover even in unpromising places. A goldcrest (above) feeds among cypress foliage while a bullfinch (right) stands by its nest.

· THE PLEASURE OF WATCHING BIRDS ·

Many people get pleasure from the birds that come into the garden. Bird-tables provide the easiest, and for many the only, way to observe wildlife. A few minutes in the garden in the evening is the perfect way to relax from the tensions of the working day.

Close encounters with wild animals are magical experiences that need not involve travel to distant parts of the globe to see the rare or exotic. The pleasure that comes from the nearness of nature can be triggered by sparrows boldly snatching proffered crumbs or a robin dropping out of a tree to pick worms from newly turned soil. Something more out of the ordinary, like a family party of long-tailed tits flitting and somersaulting through the bare twigs or a treecreeper spiralling up a

tree trunk, creates a lasting impression. The beauty of watching birds is that they live almost natural lives in the garden, allowing us the opportunity to learn some secrets of animal life. Once we have attracted birds, we want to know more about them. The question of what they do is easily answered; the questions of how

Looking for details A house sparrow brings a foot over its wing to scratch its head.

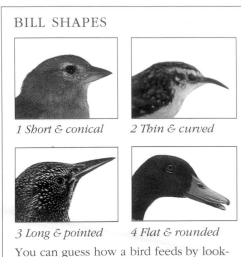

BILL SHAPES

1 Short & conical

2 Thin & curved

3 Long & pointed

4 Flat & rounded

You can guess how a bird feeds by look-ing at its bill – the chaffinch's (1) cracks seeds; the treecreeper's (2) picks up insects; the starling's (3) probes the ground; and the mallard's (4) filters water.

Long-tailed tit *If this charming bird visits your garden (often in a family group), you will appreciate its lively, entertaining behaviour, which may include special courtship flights.*

they do it and, moreover, why they do it are more difficult. Not so many years ago some of the simplest questions about the behaviour of common garden birds were baffling even to the experts. Konrad Lorenz, the Austrian naturalist who won the Nobel Prize for his pioneering studies of animal behaviour, remarked, "We must remember animals sometimes do things for which there is no reasonable explana-tion". In the 30 years or so since he made that statement, detailed studies of bird behaviour have shown that there usually

is a reasonable explanation for the things they do, although there are still some mysteries waiting to be solved.

Ornithologists have turned their attention to the habits of garden birds, setting up projects in which they have fit-ted combinations of coloured plastic rings to the legs of individual birds. After hours of patient observation, researchers have revealed many secrets of the private lives of our most familiar birds. In the process they have upset some established ideas of how we thought birds behaved.

• THE DUNNOCK'S PRIVATE LIFE •

Birdlife is proving to be much more varied and fascinating than we had previously thought. Until recently, for example, books gave the impression that the dunnock led an unexciting family life, stating that the female took the responsi-bility for building the nest and incubating the eggs and that the male stayed with her and helped feed their young. This resemblance to the human patriarchal family led a Victorian clergyman, the Rev. F.O. Morris, to write in the moralizing style typical of natural history books of

the period: "the dunnock exhibits (in de-portment and dress) a pattern which many of a higher grade might imitate, with advantage to themselves and benefit to others through an improved example".

The true state of affairs was revealed in a British study made at the Cambridge Botanic Garden. After three years' close observation, N.B. Davies concluded that it was unfortunate that the Rev. Morris had urged his readers to imitate the dunnock. The private lives of the Cambridge dun-nocks would make the storyline for a soap opera. Far from being a model of Victorian family life, dunnock society embraces not only monogamy but *polygyny* (one male mating with several females), *polyandry* (one female with several males) and *polygynandry* (several males sharing several females).

A male dunnock tries to monopolize one or, preferably, more females by guarding them against the attentions of other males. He is not always successful because the female tries to cuckold him at every opportunity. The aim of the male is to ensure that he fathers as many nest-lings as possible. Because a male dun-nock helps to feed the young of any female he has mated with, the female's aim is to mate with several males and increase the chance of her young growing up. On the other hand, she will try to prevent her partner from mating with other females because then he would be duty-bound to feed their offspring as well.

Scientific research is making our garden birds more interesting to watch. Now we know how the botanic-garden dunnocks

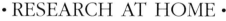

Exposed *The dunnock has regular battles of the sexes.*

behaved, we can follow the actions of those living in our own gardens. We know that when they hop across the lawn in pairs they are not showing marital fidelity but are eyeing each other jealously. If you see three dunnocks involved in a chase, you can guess that the leader is the junior male of a poly-androus trio being chased by the senior male who has caught him trying to mate with the female, who is following them.

• RESEARCH AT HOME •

Cream of the crop
In the UK, tits prefer silver tops because they cover the creamier milk.

Great tit

There is no need to be a professional scientist to carry out research on garden birds. Recently I came across the example of Dr. J.L. Crosby who reported in *The Times* his observations of tits stealing milk from foil-capped bottles. In eight days, the tits broke into 9 out of 16 silver-topped bottles containing creamy milk, but left 17 blue-topped bottles of skimmed milk. Dr. Crosby then swapped the caps on 4 bottles. The tits pierced the silver tops, realized that the milk was infe-rior and left them, but they did not have the wit to try the blue tops to look for the creamy milk they now contained. This home experiment came from the simple observation that tits opened silver tops but not blue ones. It might have been assumed that the tits found silver more attractive but it was proved that they had learnt that silver-topped bottles were actually more rewarding.

∴ THE NEED FOR GARDENS ∴

THE EROSION OF OUR countryside over the last three decades
by the dual demands of intensive agriculture and property
development means that birds need gardens to act as miniature
nature reserves. In some cases, the interests of the gardener may
clash with those of the bird-lover, although it is possible
to strike a delicate balance between the two.

· THE SUBURBANIZATION OF THE COUNTRY ·

Of the many concerns facing conserv-
ationists, the one closest to home is the
changing face of our countryside and the
effect that it has on wildlife. Not only are
rare plants and animals disappearing
altogether but familiar species, once taken
for granted, are becoming uncommon or
even rare. The countryside started to
change with the clearing of forests and
draining of swamps and marshes for
agriculture. The rate and scale of change
only increased rapidly after the Industrial
Revolution, when the human population
began its astronomic rise. Then, with the
mechanization of agriculture, came more
dramatic changes: the last 30 to 40 years
have witnessed a transformation of the

countryside that would amaze our grand-
parents. It is hard to believe the size of
bird flocks and the abundance of all kinds
of wildlife that were common in the first
half of the twentieth century. It is a
sobering thought that the robin population has decreased by 20% on farmland
in the last 10 years.

Some of the countryside has disap-
peared under bricks and mortar – partly
to house the rising human population but
also because increased affluence and
overcrowded cities have tempted people,
and their businesses, to move into rural
areas. The result is the suburbanization of
the countryside, especially where the increasing demand for building land creates

The changing countryside
With farmland scenes like this
(above) *changing, birds are
resorting to gardens* (left) *for
food and nest sites.*

a high density of houses with space for only handkerchief-sized gardens. The area covered by this new rural civilization is now seen as a haven for at least some of our beleaguered wildlife as mechanized agriculture makes even the remaining countryside less attractive.

In some gardens, wildlife is as much under threat from horticulture as from modern farming, because the passionate gardener may nurture exotic varieties of plants and flowers at the expense of everything else – plant or animal, weed or pest. The well-kept garden can be an ecological desert, where even the humble but valuable earthworm is attacked for disfiguring lawns with its casts, so it is not surprising that fruit-eating, bud-stripping birds are regarded as pests. When even that garden favourite, the blue tit, makes itself unpopular by stealing peas and blackberries, a bird has to be as innocent as the robin before it can be considered the "gardener's friend".

Garden pest
Gardeners view the bullfinch as a pest because it strips the buds from trees.

· BIRD CONSERVATION ·

Fortunately for birds, extreme dedication to growing plants is not the norm and not all householders put plants before other forms of wildlife. An increasing number of people positively encourage birds into their gardens because of the enjoyment they bring. But can we claim that managing our gardens for wildlife contributes to conservation? There is no doubt that many birds have benefited from gardens in built-up areas. Thousands of years ago, the swallow flew over rolling grasslands where it caught low-flying insects to carry back to its nest on a rock face or in a hollow tree. Buildings have given it new nesting-places and encouraged it to spread. Suburbia is now an acceptable environment for the swallow's aerial lifestyle, provided that air pollution has not killed the insects.

And, in recent years, siskins

Change of habitat
Some birds are able to adapt to new conditions: the swallow now lives over towns because buildings provide ideal nest sites.

Mouthful of insects for nestlings

New arrival *The siskin is a recent convert to the garden way of life. It is especially attracted to peanuts in red mesh bags.*

started to venture into gardens during the winter to look for food when stocks of their favourite conifer and alder seeds had been depleted. Now they are appearing regularly to feed on peanuts and fat while seed crops are still in abundant supply. In the same way, greenfinches are taking advantage of the large amounts of sunflower seeds put at their disposal in birdfeeders each winter. Instead of travelling to gardens towards the end of winter because countryside food is running out, greenfinches seem to remember that nutritious meals are easily available on bird-tables and arrive earlier each winter. The garden is no longer regarded as an emergency refuge but as a suitable environment in its own right.

· THE CHOICE OF HABITAT ·

Birds come into gardens either because they are changing their habits to make the best use of the garden environment or because various human innovations are providing them with what they need. The siskins, it seems, changed their habits to take advantage of the red mesh peanut bags that you can buy in almost all pet food shops. Mistle thrushes, on the other hand, have recently expanded into the suburbs probably because amenity tree-planting is providing them with the tall trees they need as perches when singing.

Other birds, although common in gardens, only use them as overspill areas, to be occupied when conditions deteriorate

---

THE GARDEN BIRDFEEDING SURVEY

Acorns

Ash keys

Beechnut   *Wild hazelnuts*

Research organized by the British Trust for Ornithology has shown that the numbers of nuthatches *(above)* and tits at bird-tables directly relate to the failure of crops of beechnuts and other seeds *(left).* The absence of birds in the garden is not always a sign of falling numbers. It may mean that the birds are doing well in the countryside.

in the countryside. A successful breeding season for the birds or a bad fruiting season means competition for food in their natural homes, so that some birds have to look elsewhere to live and feed. With the return of spring, the food situation eases, and these temporary visitors forsake the garden and return to the wild. That is why in one winter you might see a large number and wide variety of birds at

Common sight
One of the best-known birds in the garden, the blackbird regularly feeds on grain and stale breadcrumbs at the bird-table.

the bird-table but reduced numbers and little variety in the next. Coal tits, for instance, are particularly fickle in their attachment to gardens, staying resolutely in the woods until they have run out of food, so that in some mild winters they may not visit at all. Similarly, cold weather forces bramblings, reed buntings, redwings and fieldfares into gardens. On arrival in winter-quarters from Scandinavia, fieldfares remain nomadic, moving around the country partly at random but also being forced to move by the vagaries of weather and food supply. A cold spell makes the flocks fly off in search of food, which might lead them to your garden.

When a bird elects to stay on in a garden after the winter and nest, it would seem to have found a useful niche that provides all the objects it requires to rear a family successfully. For example, blackbirds are a common sight in the suburbs of cities, where they live at a higher density than in the surrounding countryside and where they raise more offspring. Like its cousin, the robin, the blackbird was originally a bird of woodland. It started to come into gardens a century or so ago and colonized city centres within this century. This spread was made possible partly because the blackbird is no longer persecuted for eating soft fruit, but also because suburban gardens provide the right nesting-places and food for blackbirds. (I have even seen a blackbird stealing the holly berries arranged in a Christmas wreath decorating someone's front door.)

Alternatively, the decision to live in gardens could be forced upon birds by overcrowding in the countryside. If birds cannot find enough nesting-space in their usual environment, a garden will provide a second-best territory. When a hard winter wipes out large numbers of wrens, the survivors live mostly in woods and on the banks of streams, so we can conclude that the garden is only a wren's second choice of environment. There is also evidence that blue and great tits, which initially seem such perfect garden birds, do not breed so well in gardens as they do in woodland. They lay fewer eggs and rear fewer young because of a shortage of their preferred spiders and caterpillars.

But whether your garden is a bird's first or second choice to live in, it is clear that gardens are definitely a better place for birds than land given over to intensive agriculture or high-density building. Even if gardens seem to compare unfavourably with woodlands, tree-lined streams and other natural features of the countryside, there are many different ways in which you can try to make your garden as attractive a habitat for birds as possible.

∴ GARDENING FOR BIRDS ∵

THE PROVISION OF FOOD and places for birds to nest, drink and bathe, as described in *Attracting Birds*, ensures that some birds will visit your garden. More time, money and commitment are required if you want to make it a favourable habitat for as many birds as possible. It is easy enough to put up a bird-table on the lawn and nest-boxes in trees. It is another matter to plan, landscape and plant a bird garden to encourage birds.

· BIRDS AND PLANTS ·

It is not worthwhile creating a bird garden if your space outside is a playground for cats or small children. Also, you may find it difficult to attract birds if you wish to remain a fussy gardener. A first-rate garden for birds is likely to be more over-grown than a serious gardener would allow. For instance, it is hardly usual hor-ticultural practice to leave groundsel and thistles to seed, but that is how you can attract goldfinches. A tidy garden does not provide the best opportunities for birds to find food and shelter. Indeed, if they do come across food, there is every chance the birds will be branded as pests.

Too often, gardeners aim to destroy as many insects, snails, slugs and woodlice as possible. Apart from the danger to birds that eat poisoned pests, a shortage of insects will cause infant deaths among birds. Remember that birds especially need insects and other animal food when feeding their young. A profusion of vege-tation encourages the insects needed for

Two ways to attract birds
Setting up bird-tables and baths (above) is an easy way to tempt birds to visit. But to create a bird garden (left), you may need to modify your outlook on horticulture.

successful nesting, but no-one pursuing horticultural excellence will grow brassicas as a nursery for caterpillars. Unfortunately, you cannot rely on birds to control insect pests for you. If anything, it is the other way round – the number of insects controls the number of birds. If blue tits attack greenfly on your roses it can mean two things: either other food is so scarce that tits are eating these tiny insects as a last resort, or there is such a plague of greenfly that even the tits' feasts will not eradicate them.

Golden opportunity
Grow teazels for the brilliant goldfinch.

· IDEAL BIRD GARDENS ·

The best plan for any bird garden is to settle on a reasonable compromise. Only the keenest bird-gardener plants clumps of sedges to encourage nesting sedge warblers or knocks holes in the house to accommodate swifts' nests. However, a careful choice of plants to stock the garden and a suitable regime of cultivation with, for instance, a little judicious laziness in weeding and tidying, create an environment

Animal food
Birds, such as tits, eat the insects that feed on plants.

Blue tit

that attracts a wide range of bird species without making the garden unsightly. The best bird gardens are those that have been in existence for several decades. They are well-established, their trees and shrubs are mature and time has dismissed the well-manicured look. Such gardens are often as near perfect for birds as possible because of their variety. Herbaceous borders, a kitchen garden and a lawn, as well as outhouses, old walls and log piles, provide useful nooks and crannies for nesting and roosting, or enable birds to forage for a range of foods. Increasingly, however, people are living in new houses, which may be built on single plots (perhaps carved out from the large gardens of houses built in a more expansive age), or on new estates built in the countryside. The latter type of garden often starts only as an enclosure of bare soil churned by building contractors' vehicles, although it may have a head-start by incorporating an old field hedge or a mature tree.

Leatherjackets
These cranefly larvae, which feed on the roots of grasses, are much appreciated by rooks and starlings.

Grasshoppers *These plant-eating insects are eaten by many birds, including little owls and wrens.*

GARDENING FOR BIRDS

If you do own a brand-new plot of churned-up mud and builders' rubble, what can you do to attract birds, apart from set up a bird-table or bird-bath and position an assortment of nest-boxes in trees or on the sides of sheds? Although not worth the effort if you are planning to move home for a new job or better

location, the creation of a bird garden is within the reach of everyone with an interest in birds. It is largely a matter of choosing the right plants and letting the garden grow a little wild. The difference with a wildlife garden is merely one of emphasis, in that the planning should take into account the needs of birds and other wildlife without ignoring the traditional ingredients of a garden, such as trees, hedges, shrubs, a lawn and flowerbeds.

Several specialist books give practical details for creating a wildlife garden that will attract birds. Even though they concentrate on growing wild plants and encouraging insects, these are precisely the features that will make a garden a first-rate place for birds.

Bird's-eye view This neat garden includes all the traditional elements – only a slight change of emphasis, such as allowing clovers and dandelions to grow in the lawn, is needed to convert it into a more bird-friendly habitat.

· TREES ·

Established trees are the most important features for the majority of garden birds and are vital for treecreepers, nuthatches and woodpeckers. Assuming that you have room for a tree and want to make a long-term investment, choose one that supports plenty of insects, as well as fruit. Native trees are best: oak heads the list

(sheltering around 300 insect species), followed in order by willow, birch and hawthorn. Goat (or pussy) willow makes a quick-growing screen and its catkins attract the first insects of spring, providing valuable food for insectivorous birds, including early warblers. Blue tits even sip the nectar. These and other trees, such as

Importance of trees Some birds are unlikely to venture into gardens unless they contain mature trees.

Nuthatch with a mouthful of food

Treecreeper with an assortment of caterpillars

beech, ash, alder and hazel, also have valuable crops of seeds or fruit. Conifers such as pine, spruce and larch not only provide year-round shelter from predators but also contain seeds in their cones and insects among their needles. They are especially popular with goldcrests.

Trees that produce fruit in autumn and winter include wild cherry, rowan and elder, which are quickly stripped. The apple tree is perhaps the most useful tree in the garden: if left unsprayed, it supports a wide selection of insects. It has ornamental blossom, which can be shared with bullfinches, and edible fruit, with which you can entice a variety of birds in autumn and winter.

Cherry blossom *Insects feeding on the nectar from the masses of blossom in spring draw insectivorous birds to your garden.*

EDIBLE SEEDS

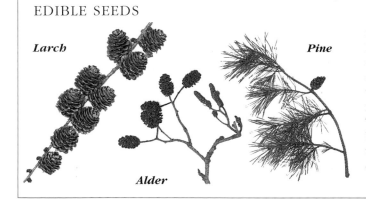

Larch

Pine

Alder

If you are lucky enough to have mature, native trees (especially conifers or oaks) in your garden, then you can anticipate visits from a variety of birdlife. Their seeds attract a number of species, including tits, woodpeckers, siskins, crossbills and greenfinches.

• HEDGES •

A hedge, consisting of closely planted and pruned trees and shrubs, provides protection from overhead predators, and nest sites for many birds. If you encourage the undergrowth, a hedge gives shelter to dunnocks and wrens. Hawthorn is the prize hedge plant because of its fast-growing and robust habit but holly, yew

Wild hedge *If you can tolerate the look of an untended hedge, let plants, such as hawthorn, oak and holly, grow naturally to provide food as well as cover for roosting and nesting.*

Hawthorn fruits *Only borne on unclipped hedges, the fleshy fruits provide winter food for blackbirds, fieldfares and redwings.*

Ferrying food *A wren has gathered insects from a hedge for its young nestlings.*

and wild privet are close runners-up that may provide a rich supply of berries. If clipped, these plants will not produce flowers or fruit, but the occasional plant can be left to grow up into a hedgerow tree, and diversity can be added to the hedge by including a hazel or blackthorn.

· SHRUBS ·

Shrubs are useful for shelter and most have berries, which are choice bird food. Particularly suitable plants are black-berries (especially when allowed to grow into a thicket), pyracantha, mahonia and elder. Walls and fences can support climbing shrubs, like ivy, honeysuckle, cotoneaster and berberis. Ivy is valuable because it flowers and fruits late in the year, providing food in late winter. The cotoneaster (useful against a shaded wall) is a lure for winter waxwings, while the prickly berberis, as well as providing berries, may entice long-tailed tits to nest.

Food and shelter *Shrubs shield the ground from snow. A bird's footprints (above) lead into the clear patch where food is to be found. A range of plants (left) entices a range of birds. Birds feed on the insects that ivy flowers (right) attract in autumn, and eat ivy berries in winter.*

· THE LAWN ·

The lawn is a valuable hunting-ground for many birds. Thrushes, blackbirds and starlings peer and probe for worms and leatherjackets. Watch their contrasting styles: thrushes and blackbirds hunt stealthily, hopping and pausing to watch for prey, while starlings stride about industriously, thrusting their bills deep into the ground and dragging out their quarry. You may also see dunnocks and pied wagtails picking up small insects, and, most exciting of all, a green woodpecker probing for ants.

Watering your lawn in dry weather brings earthworms to the surface and birds to the garden; worms are a great boon when there are nestlings to feed. If you postpone mowing the lawn for long enough, dandelions will produce seeds for finches, some woodpigeons may come to feed on clover plants and, later, bullfinches come down to eat their seeds. You can leave the lawn to grow around trees and, although this will be less useful to the worm-hunters, long grass shelters many other kinds of small animal for the birds to find, while the grasses, thistles, groundsel, knapweed and other weeds there will set seed for finches.

Natural supplies Your lawn turf harbours a hidden stock of bird food (below).

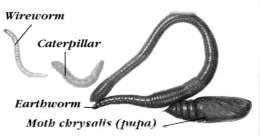

Wireworm

Caterpillar

Earthworm

Moth chrysalis (pupa)

Diet of worms *A song thrush* (left) *pecks an earthworm to subdue it. The thrush catches worms with fast, sharp strikes and pulls them from their burrows in the lawn.*

· FLOWERBEDS ·

Flowerbeds offer a great feeding-place for insect-eaters, like robins and dunnocks, and seed-eaters, like the chaffinch, while a layer of mulch or compost is soon scattered by a blackbird flicking through it for worms and insects. Border plants are not rich food sources for birds but some varieties can be useful. A cascade of aubrieta, for example, supports the first crop of aphids, while snapdragons and pansies provide seeds for bullfinches, and a good-sized clump of teazels attracts goldfinches. If you have room in your garden, leave an odd corner for some useful weeds to set seed, such as knotgrass, sowthistle and stinging nettle (which also attracts butterflies).

Bedfellows *A robin and a house sparrow explore the edge of a flowerbed for any food they can find. The freshly turned soil yields a rich stock of animal and vegetable food.*

∴ WHO'S IN THE GARDEN? ∵

THE VARIETY OF BIRDS that frequents a garden depends on its locality. For instance, there will be many more regular visitors to a rural garden than one in a city centre. The number and type of birds that visit a rural garden depend on the nature of the surrounding countryside (for example, whether it is woodland, farmland or marshland) as well as the season.

· THE VARIETY OF BIRDLIFE ·

I used to live on the west coast of Scotland and often saw a dipper or heron in the stream that ran through my garden, while a buzzard occasionally perched on the fence and woodcocks regularly flew over on summer evenings. Herring, lesser black-backed and common gulls nesting in the surrounding hills visited my bird-table, but house sparrows and starlings stayed away. Later, when in eastern England, my garden birds included moorhens, corn buntings, pheasants and red-legged partridges from the surrounding farmland, as well as house martins.

The kinds of bird that will visit your garden depend on where you live, but there is always the possibility of uncommon or rare birds appearing, including

Lesser black-backed gull Local areas have their own pattern of birdlife. I sometimes saw this close relative of the herring gull taking scraps from the bird-table in my garden in west Scotland.

accidental visitors knocked off-course by severe weather when migrating. Well over 100 species of bird have been recorded eating food put out for them at feeders in British gardens. Some individual gardens have been visited by as many as 40–50 different visitors each.

Birds to watch for Among the many birds that sometimes come into gardens, the moorhen (above) *may creep in from nearby streams, while a garden pond is an attraction for a heron* (left), *which comes to steal fish.*

·COMMON VISITORS·

An "average" garden is visited, on a regular basis, by 15–20 species of bird, although there are generally fewer visitors to towns compared to the countryside. These will be the most common birds, but the garden will also have occasional visits from perhaps another 10 species, depending on its situation.

Common European garden birds were the subject of a survey set up by the British Trust for Ornithology in the winter of 1987–8. It was noted that a total of 118 species visited 293 gardens in countries from Finland to Portugal. The top 12 most frequent visitors were: great tit, blackbird, house sparrow, blue tit, robin, chaffinch, greenfinch, magpie, tree sparrow, collared dove, wren and dunnock. There were regional variations: for example, in British gardens starling and song thrush replaced tree sparrow and wren in the top 12.

Another, more recent, birdwatch on the weekend of 28/29 January 1989 had slightly different results. The research, carried out by the Young Ornithologists' Club (the junior section of the Royal Society for the Protection of Birds), discovered that the top 10 birds in British gardens and parks were, in order of abundance: starling, house sparrow, blue tit, blackbird, gulls (species not recorded), chaffinch, robin, greenfinch, great tit and crow. Similar watches were carried out in other countries around the world at the same time. Once again, the results for the other countries in

western Europe were similar to the British list, although they did reflect some geographical differences.

Within each country, every garden will have its own species list depending on its particular location. For instance, the wren and coal tit are much more likely to come into gardens that contain conifers, while the nuthatch and great spotted woodpecker need to find a habitat that includes mature, broad-leaved trees.

Top-ten bird The chaffinch is a common visitor to gardens everywhere.

Newcomer Once a rare bird in Europe, the collared dove has spread rapidly to become one of the most common garden birds.

· VISITORS THROUGH THE YEAR ·

There are three categories of bird that will visit your garden: winter visitors, summer breeders and birds of passage, which pass through on migration in spring and autumn. There is some overlap, especially between the summer and winter residents, because the common tits, robins, blackbirds and others that used the bird-table in winter may stake out territories in your garden and stay to

nest. Nevertheless, you should still be able to detect a definite change in the garden's birdlife through the seasons.

At the end of winter, some garden birds disappear, either migrating to distant breeding-grounds, like the fieldfare and redwing, or merely returning to the countryside, like the reed bunting and some of the wrens and tits. They are replaced by the summer visitors, such as the spotted

Garden timetables *The drab-looking spotted flycatcher, feeding its young in a garden shed* (left), *is one of the latest visitors to arrive in summer, while you may see the pied wagtail* (below) *all year round in gardens.*

Year-round species *The sparrowhawk is naturally a bird of woodland and hedgerows. It is now the bird of prey that is most commonly seen in gardens.*

flycatcher, house martin and swallow. While winter brings a flow of birds into the garden in search of food, territorial behaviour limits the numbers in spring and summer, so birds may disappear. One year I watched birds singing and courting in my garden, then gathering nest material, but all, with the exception of a pair of starlings in a nest-box, built their nests in neighbouring gardens. (The consolation was that when the young birds started to fly, they often came into my garden with their parents to feed.)

Between winter and summer, there are two other interesting periods when birds pass through the garden, on migration. In late summer and autumn, garden birdlife is supplemented by newly independent birds, which spread around the country in search of homes of their own. All sorts of birds may turn up at these times, so a special watch is worthwhile. In spring, you may see warblers, such as chiffchaffs and willow warblers, searching the roses for early greenfly before they move on to their nesting-grounds. You can recognize these migrants more easily after breeding (from July or August onwards) because they sing intermittently when they stop over in the garden to fatten up before setting out on their long return journeys.

Spring moves The chiffchaff (above), *an early arrival, may nest in a garden with dense shrubs. After winter, the reed bunting* (left) *leaves the garden to nest in wet places.*

· RARE VISITORS ·

Almost every kind of bird has been seen in gardens. If escaped cage-birds are included, the list contains parrots, canaries and waxbills. The migration season also provides some incredible strangers that have strayed far off-course. Garden records include little auks (seabirds related to the puffin, which breed in the Arctic but normally winter at sea in the North Atlantic), myrtle warblers, which must have flown non-stop from America, and bitterns forced out of reedbeds by icy weather. There is no knowing what may turn up: it could be a budgerigar from down the road or the first European record for an exotic species, like the American golden-winged warbler that took up residence in 1988 on a housing estate in southern England. It was visited by over 3,000 birdwatchers from across Europe.

If a strange bird does appear in your garden, record the details of its appearance and try to find a birdwatcher to confirm its identification before it disappears. If it is a genuine rarity, be prepared to play host to hordes of bird-enthusiasts. I remember meeting a crowd outside a cottage because word had spread that there was a rare rose-coloured starling feeding in the garden with a flock of its common cousins. At intervals, someone would kindly throw out more crusts to tempt the starlings back into the garden.

Budgerigars
These small parrots, kept as pets, are the commonest escapees.

∴ BIRDS IN TOWNS ∴

Watching birds in urban gardens may be a poor substitute for going into the countryside, but you can nevertheless widen your birdwatching horizons by stepping outside the garden gate. If you have merely a postage stamp-size garden, or no garden at all, you will still be able to find plenty of birds not only in parks and squares but also in any waste ground awaiting development and other open spaces in towns and cities.

· URBAN BIRDWATCHING ·

There has been increasing interest in urban wildlife in recent years as more town-dwellers have become concerned about their surroundings. Positive attempts are being made to prevent the total swamping of the urban environment with tarmac and concrete, and to preserve wildlife in workplaces and recreational areas, as well as private gardens. Many birds are finding built-up areas acceptable living-places. There are even some advantages to city life: the air temperature is a few degrees warmer than in the country – a great comfort on winter nights – and streetlights let birds feed for longer. The chief benefit with resident city birds is that they are tolerant of humans so you can easily approach them to practise identification and study their habits.

City cormorant
A cormorant preens as it dries off. You may see this wide-spread seabird, distinguished by its upright stance and black plumage, on park lakes.

Hand-out *Familiarity with humans makes some species hand-tame.*

House sparrows

· CITY CENTRES ·

A park with mature trees supports plenty of bird species, while a stretch of open water, whether a river, canal, ornamental lake, reservoir or flooded gravel pit, contains the widest variety of birds. Only in the worst inner-city environments, with hardly a patch of greenery, are there few opportunities for birds. Even there, house sparrows, starlings and street pigeons (and perhaps jackdaws and gulls) will be in evidence – species that nest on buildings and glean food from the litter that accumulates in unkempt streets and squares. These birds may become a problem for the civic authorities because their fouling poses possible health hazards. The larger birds create an extra nuisance by emptying the contents of litterbins or ripping open refuse bags, left out for collection, in their search for food.

Inner-city species adapt their behaviour to their proximity with humans. House sparrows, as the name suggests, are the birds most at home in inner cities. Railway stations and warehouses sometimes have resident sparrow populations that remain under cover, never flying into open air from one generation to the next. Pigeons are so bold in walking among people's feet that the flocks gathering in public places become tourist attractions, despite attempts by town authorities to limit their numbers. The amazing phenomenon of the urban roosting of starlings is often overlooked: as darkness gathers, starlings stream in from feeding-grounds, 15 or more miles away, to gather in their thousands on trees and buildings, filling the air with their whistling and chattering.

High-density housing estates, which were a chief feature of urban development in the 1960s and 1970s, make conditions for birds almost as hostile as

Communal bathing *A group of street pigeons bathe at the edge of a park lake and wash the grime of the city from their feathers.*

in city centres. Bare lawns with a few scattered trees fill the spaces between buildings and there are no thickly planted gardens or shrubberies to provide food and cover. Only a few additional species will want to nest in these conditions; perhaps scattered pairs of blackbirds and blue tits will find small corners where something approximating the natural world retains a hold.

City sights *A rook eats leftovers from a rubbish bag* (above) *while starlings stand by. The herring gull* (right) *nests on buildings, annoying occupiers with its fouling and noise.*

· COLONIZATION OF TOWNS ·

As new buildings sprawl over the country-side and pockets of untouched land are overtaken by development, the variety of birdlife diminishes. The species that disappear are those that need either woodland or wide, open spaces. The first naturalists to record the effects of the growing towns made pessimistic forecasts that these birds would die out or become rarities. As it is, a surprising number of birds have held their ground and adjusted to town life, and some birds have un-expectedly established themselves.

The urban sprawl of Greater London is home to over 50 breeding species, although not all nest every year. London does well for birds because of the large area occupied by the parks near its centre. Twenty-one nesting species and a further 40 non-breeders were discovered in a survey of the grounds of Buckingham Palace (an unusually large town garden!). But far less exclusive places have also had their triumphs, such as the nesting of a pair of yellow wagtails at the site of the old Surrey Docks in East London.

Town bird *Within this century, the black redstart has gradually spread through Europe and established itself in towns.*

Derelict land, where buildings have been demolished, also provides good opportu-nities for urban birds, perhaps because it supports plentiful crops of weeds and it is relatively undisturbed. This is the apparent reason for the colonization of central London by the black redstart. The first record of black redstarts nesting in London came in 1926. Numbers increased from 1942 when redstarts began to appear on bomb sites: the ruined buildings

Life among the litter *A coot passes a twig to its mate as they build their nest on a rubbish-strewn city canal. The birds are less bothered by the unsightly litter than we are.*

provided them with crevices and ledges for their nests and they fed on midges emerging from pools and streams. When rebuilding started after the Second World War, the black redstarts dwindled in number until they moved to industrial sites, such as power stations, railway sidings and warehouses. Since then, the population has continued to flourish.

Other interesting birds have spread into city centres. The reduction of air pollution achieved by outlawing the emission of smoke has encouraged insect life so that swifts, swallows and martins can hunt overhead and nest on buildings. Ledges on buildings are also used as nest sites by kestrels, which feed on sparrows, as do tawny owls in parks and suburbs. Over

Urban scavenger *A young black-headed gull spends its first winter in a town. It will probably return to a coastal site to breed.*

the last century, gulls, especially the black-headed gull, have become urban birds, replacing the scavenging kites and ravens of previous years. Some have formed inland colonies, and herring gulls regularly nest on buildings (p.27). While inland, they roost at reservoirs or gravel pits on the outskirts of the city and commute in daily to feed.

Suburban resident *A tawny owl, often seen in parks and leafy suburbs, swallows a mouse.*

· INLAND WATERS ·

By far the best place for watching town birds is from the banks of park lakes, reservoirs, flooded gravel pits, rivers or canals. Mute swans, mallards, moorhens and coots are common, with the first three often tame enough to be fed on scraps. There may also be reed buntings and sedge warblers, if there is a suitable fringe of reeds. Occasionally you may see a kingfisher where water has remained unpolluted. Herons also come to feed on inland waters and have established nesting colonies in London, Amsterdam and other European cities. The main interest for birdwatchers is the birds that visit open waters in winter. Flotillas of ducks gather to roost in safety and, among the common tufted ducks, teal and pochard, as well as Canada geese, you may spot rarer visitors such as red-throated divers, white-fronted geese or smew (ducks that fly in from the USSR for the winter).

Lucky sight *The beautiful kingfisher is a prize bird to see by lakes or canals. It perches on branches before diving to catch small fish.*

CHAPTER TWO

BIRD PROFILES

BIRDS CAN BE enjoyed simply for their colour, movement or song, but anyone with a degree of curiosity wants to know which birds are visiting their garden. Confident identification is essential, for instance, if the details of birds' habits in *Behaviour Guide* are to make sense. The directory of bird profiles is a superb means of identifying most of the common (and a few less common) species that you may spot in a garden or park and describes their typical feeding and nesting habits. In particular, guidance is given, wherever possible, for distinguishing sexes and age groups. It makes it more interesting if you realize that the brownish blackbird being chased across the lawn, for example, is a young male rather than a female because it explains the intent of the glossy, black adult male that is giving chase.

A young treecreeper camouflaged against a tree

∵ WHAT BIRD IS THAT? ∵

T HE PURPOSE OF *Bird Profiles* is to introduce a representative
selection of common birds and describe their habits so that
they become familiar figures in the garden. This reference guide
will be of most help to those readers with little experience of
birdwatching but who want to play host to birds in their garden
and are keen to put names to faces. If you know what to look
for, you are bound to have success in identifying birds.

· POSITIVE IDENTIFICATION ·

There are two possible ways to identify
an unknown bird. You can either thumb
through a bird book until you find the
picture of a likely candidate or you can
ask a knowledgable birdwatcher. Both
ways only work if you observe the bird
carefully and note the key features that
will confirm its identity. Otherwise, the
book will present a bewildering kaleido-
scope of birds, which look almost, but not
quite, like the one you saw. And the birdwatcher will not be able to match your
vague description with the pictures in his
mental field guide. Make notes of a bird's
size and obvious physical features but

also record details, such as voice, flight
pattern, posture at rest, how the bird
walks and where it was seen.

I was once stumped by a request to
name a "black and white" bird. I worked
through magpie, pied wagtail, long-tailed
tit and spotted woodpecker – but none
was right. Finally the puzzle was solved
by the clue that the bird was seen flying
away from fruit bushes. What was
glimpsed was a bullfinch! – from behind,
its black cap, back and tail contrasted
with its white rump. Once realized, it was
obvious, but I would have got there
quicker if I had been given its rough size.

THE PARTS OF A BIRD'S BODY

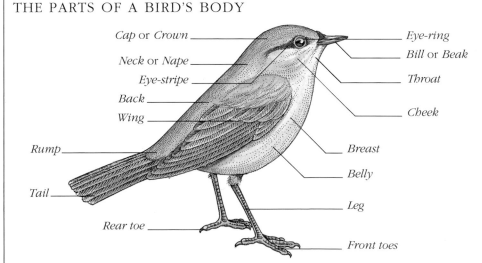

Cap or Crown

Neck or Nape

Eye-stripe

Back

Wing

Rump

Tail

Rear toe

Eye-ring

Bill or Beak

Throat

Cheek

Breast

Belly

Leg

Front toes

Recording the details Use the names above
when taking notes. Trace over the drawing so
you have an outline that you can quickly fill in
with details of your mystery bird. Register its
colours and the size, shape and colour of the

bill and legs. Look carefully at any stripe on
the face: does it run through the eye or above
it? It is important to judge the bird's size: compare it with known birds, such as sparrows or
starlings, or else a leaf or a brick in a wall.

· THE BIRD PROFILE ·

Forty-five bird species are listed here within their family groups, according to the conventional order of scientific classification (p.189). Both the common and scientific names of the family and species are given. Any significant features of each bird are described in detail for ease of identification. The information provided on feeding and nesting will help you meet the needs of particular birds.

Family group

Scientific name of family

Common name

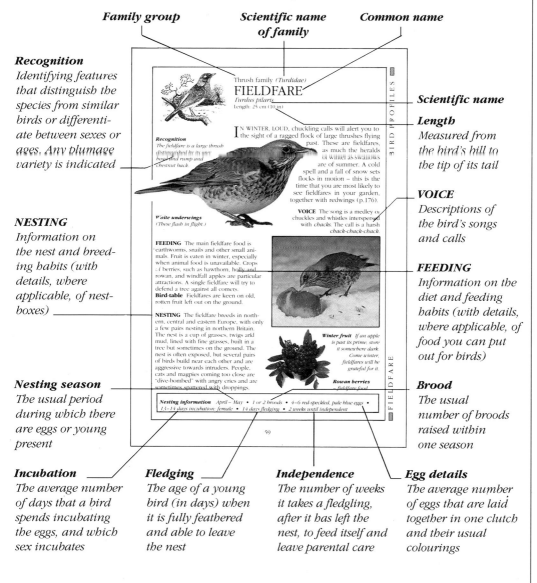

Recognition
Identifying features that distinguish the species from similar birds or differenti- ate between sexes or ages. Any plumage variety is indicated

NESTING
Information on the nest and breed- ing habits (with details, where applicable, of nest- boxes)

Nesting season
The usual period during which there are eggs or young present

Scientific name

Length
Measured from the bird's bill to the tip of its tail

VOICE
Descriptions of the bird's songs and calls

FEEDING
Information on the diet and feeding habits (with details, where applicable, of food you can put out for birds)

Brood
The usual number of broods raised within one season

Inside the profile illustration:

Thrush family *(Turdidae)*
FIELDFARE
Turdus pilaris
Length: 25 cm (10 in)

IN WINTER, LOUD, chuckling calls will alert you to the sight of a ragged flock of large thrushes flying past. These are fieldfares, as much the heralds of winter as swallows are of summer. A cold spell and a fall of snow sets flocks in motion – this is the time that you are most likely to see fieldfares in your garden, together with redwings (p.176).

Recognition *The fieldfare is a large thrush distinguished by its grey head and rump and chestnut back.*

Voice underwings *(These flash in flight.)*

VOICE The song is a medley of chuckles and whistles interspersed with *chacks*. The call is a harsh *chack-chack-chack*.

FEEDING The main fieldfare food is earthworms, snails and other small ani- mals. Fruit is eaten in winter, especially when animal food is unavailable. Crops of berries, such as hawthorn, holly and rowan, and windfall apples are particular attractions. A single fieldfare will try to defend a tree against all comers.
Bird-table Fieldfares are keen on old, rotten fruit left out on the ground.

NESTING The fieldfare breeds in north- ern, central and eastern Europe, with only a few pairs nesting in northern Britain. The nest is a cup of grasses, twigs and mud, lined with fine grasses, built in a tree but sometimes on the ground. The nest is often exposed, but several pairs of birds build near each other and are aggressive towards intruders. People, cats and magpies coming too close are "dive-bombed" with angry cries and are sometimes spattered with droppings.

Winter fruit *If an apple is past its prime, store it somewhere dark. Come winter, fieldfares will be grateful for it.*

Rowan berries *– fieldfare food*

Nesting information April – May • 1 or 2 broods • 4–6 red-speckled, pale blue eggs • 13–14 days incubation: female • 14 days fledging • 2 weeks until independent

59

Incubation
The average number of days that a bird spends incubating the eggs, and which sex incubates

Fledging
The age of a young bird (in days) when it is fully feathered and able to leave the nest

Independence
The number of weeks it takes a fledgling, after it has left the nest, to feed itself and leave parental care

Egg details
The average number of eggs that are laid together in one clutch and their usual colourings

Nesting information The figures (placed in the box at the bottom of the page) for brood and egg numbers, and incubation, fledging and independence times are only approx- imate. They are likely to vary, depending on circumstances. For example, first-time breeders tend to lay fewer eggs than the average range indicated above. The availability of food is another important factor that influences the size of a clutch of eggs (pp.156–7).

Heron family *(Ardeidae)*

GREY HERON
Ardea cinerea
Length: 90 cm (36 in)

THE HERON IS a wary bird that rarely comes into the garden but steals fish or frogs from ponds when it does. Once a heron has found the source of an easy meal, it is likely to return until it has cleaned out the pond. Unless you make a special point of keeping watch when it sneaks in at dawn or dusk, you will spot one only if it is disturbed, as it rises steeply to make a hurried escape.

Black plumes

Dagger-like bill

Recognition
The heron is a very large bird with long legs and neck.

Grey plumage above

White underneath

FEEDING The heron mainly eats fish, amphibians and large insects, but also small mammals and other animals.
Bird-table Assorted meat scraps are sometimes taken in hard weather.

Flight *The grey heron flies on broad wings with head held in and legs trailing.*

Pond robber *A heron swallows a goldfish.*

VOICE The most common call that you are likely to hear is a harsh *fraank*.

NESTING The heron nests in tall trees (rarely on buildings), usually alongside several other nests in a *heronry*, which may be hundreds of years old. The nest, which consists of a large platform of twigs, is built by both sexes and lined with grass. The heronry is often used as a communal winter roost. Breeding starts early in the year, with most of the eggs being laid by early April.

Nesting information   *February – July   •   1 brood   •   4 or 5 pale blue eggs   •   25–26 days incubation: both sexes   •   50 days fledging   •   2–3 weeks until independent*

Duck family *(Anatidae)*
MALLARD
Anas platyrhynchos
Length: 58 cm (23 in)

P ROBABLY ONE OF the best-known birds, the mallard is the ancestor of almost all domestic ducks. It visits rural gardens where there is a pond, or if the garden is near a lake or river. Mallards may nest in large gardens that have plenty of cover. The female may need your help in leading her ducklings safely across roads to water.

Recognition *A white ring separates the* drake's *(male's) bottle-green head from his breast.*

Plumage After the male has accompanied the female to the nest, he moults into the *eclipse* plumage, similar to the female's brown, mottled plumage (*below*). Ducks shed all their flight-feathers at once and become flightless. After the breeding season, males moult back into their brilliant colouring.

MALE

Wing-patch (speculum) – *bright blue or purple, edged with black and white, on both sexes*

FEMALE

VOICE There is a variety of quacks made. The female emits a harsh series of quacks, whereas the male has quieter, nasal quacks.

FEEDING Mallards eat a wide range of food; watch them grazing on lawns, eating acorns and hunting for water-snails, caddis fly larvae, frogs or fish in shallow water. Ducklings feed mainly on insects.
Bird-table Mallards take bread and grain in parks and gardens.

NESTING The nest of leaves and grasses is placed under dense vegetation, sometimes in a tree. The female, who rears the family by herself, covers the nest with down when she leaves to feed. The eggs hatch together and the ducklings depart the nest before they are a day old.
Nest-box Large enclosed box (p.115).

Insulation Eggs are kept warm by downy feathers.

Nesting information *March – October • 1 brood • 8–12 grey-green eggs • 27–28 days incubation: female • 50–60 days fledging • Independent at fledging*

Falcon family *(Falconidae)*

KESTREL

Falco tinnunculus

Length: 34 cm (13¹/₂ in)

Grey head

Male *The adult male has a grey head and tail. (The female has a barred black and brown tail.)*

Pointed wings

Streaked breast

I N RECENT YEARS the kestrel was the bird of prey most often seen around gardens until the sparrowhawk population recovered from widespread pesticide poisoning. The kestrel is the easier bird to recognize because of its habit of floating in a stiff breeze or hovering in the air with rapidly whirring wings. Although strenuous, hovering allows the kestrel to cover wide areas when scanning for prey on the ground.

Recognition *The kestrel can be distinguished from the sparrowhawk (p.24) by its more pointed wings and streaked breast.*

Mouse

VOICE During the breeding season, listen for a shrill *kee-kee-kee*.

FEEDING The main prey is rodents, large insects and earthworms, but kestrels may ambush small birds by dashing behind hedges, like a sparrowhawk.
Bird-table Meat scraps, and even fat and biscuits, are taken on rare occasions.

Remains *Bones of rodents are regurgitated in a pellet.*

NESTING No nest is built but a lining of sticks and straw may be added to a hole in a tree, an old nest or a ledge on cliffs and buildings.
Nest-box Open-fronted nest-box (p.115).

Bird of prey *A juvenile kestrel tears beakfuls of flesh from a mouse.*

Nesting information *April – July • 1 brood • 4 or 5 brown-blotched, white eggs •
27–29 days incubation: female • 27–32 days fledging • 4 weeks until independent*

Pheasant family *(Phasianidae)*

PHEASANT

Phasianus colchicus
Length: Male 84 cm (33 in); Female 58 cm (23 in)

THE ROMANS CARRIED the pheasant through Europe from Asia and it was introduced to Britain by the Normans. It enters gardens usually in autumn and winter, especially in hard weather. You are more likely to see cock pheasants because the females keep to the woods. As with other birds in which the male is colourful and the female dull, the female is wholly responsible for raising the family.

Dark green head
Red face

Recognition *Whether magnificently copper-coloured like this male or drab brown like the female (below right), a pheasant cannot be confused with any other bird in the garden.*

MALE

Foraging
A male pecks at the ground for grain. Some individuals have a white neck-ring.

VOICE
The male's song is a loud *kork-kok*, which the female replies to with a *kea, kea*. There is a *kut-ok, kut-ok* of alarm. The female has a variety of calls that causes her brood to hide.

FEEDING Pheasants scratch for a wide range of foods, especially grain and other seeds and acorns, and clamber in trees for buds and fruit. Animal food includes insects, snails, worms and occasionally small mammals and lizards. Grass, leaves and roots are eaten in winter.

Bird-table Pheasants eat grain, bread and kitchen leftovers.

NESTING The female nests in a shallow depression, under a hedge or in long grass or bracken. The chicks leave the nest shortly after hatching.

Camouflage *A female incubating the eggs in her nest on the ground blends perfectly with the surrounding dead bracken.*

Nesting information *March – July • 1 brood • 8–15 olive-brown eggs • 23–28 days incubation: female • 12 days fledging • 9–10 weeks until independent*

37

Rail family *(Rallidae)*

MOORHEN
Gallinula chloropus
Length: 33 cm (13 in)

THE MOORHEN IS most often seen in parks, where it stalks daintily across the grass around lakes, but a garden pond also entices and, if there is enough cover, a moorhen may nest there. Watch for moorhens in trees: they are surprisingly agile and regularly roost on branches. Young moorhens of the first brood stay with their parents and help feed their younger siblings of the second.

Red bill and shield (absent in young)

White feathers under tail

White line on flank

FEEDING The moorhen takes small animals, such as worms, snails and fish, and a variety of leaves, seeds and berries.
Bird-table Bread and fat on the ground.

Breadwinner A moorhen (right) eats a crust.

VOICE A loud, sharp *purruk* often gives away the moorhen's presence.

Toes Moorhens fight fierce territorial battles with their feet and, as a result, can easily end up with broken toes.

NESTING The nest is constructed from twigs and dead reeds among water vegetation (p.153), but also in hedges or trees, and is lined with finer plants. The male gathers most of the material while the female builds the nest. If the water level rises during incubation, more material is added to lift the eggs clear.

Chick A two-week old moorhen finds its own food but receives extra rations from its parents.

Nesting information *April – August • 2 or 3 broods • 5– 8 dark-spotted, buff eggs •
21–22 days incubation: both sexes • 40–50 days fledging • 1– 7 weeks until independent*

Rail family *(Rallidae)*

COOT
Fulica atra
Length: 38 cm (15 in)

White shield on face *(missing when young)*

COMPARED WITH ITS relative, the moorhen, the coot is a more aquatic species that prefers larger ponds and lakes, even slow-flowing rivers. This makes it less likely to come into gardens but it is common in parks and on urban reservoirs. Watch for conflicts between rivals, in which one coot races after another over the water or fights by sitting back on its tail and kicking and clawing. Sometimes a flock unites to drive away a gull or hawk by kicking up a shower of water.

VOICE A loud *kowk* is the most common of a number of calls.

Fishing *A coot eats a stickleback. Before diving, coots squeeze air from their plumage to decrease their buoyancy.*

Fleshy lobes on toes – *a swimming aid*

FEEDING Water plants, fish and animals, such as snails, beetles and bugs, are brought up from the bottom of ponds, or stolen from swans and ducks. Small mammals and birds may be taken on land.
Bird-table Although rare garden feeders, coots eat scraps, bread and grain.

Pond food *The coot eats a broad variety of small animals and plant food found in water.*

Great ramshorn snail shell

Fool's watercress ╱ **Hornwort**

NESTING The nest is a pile of vegetation built in shallow water. The male collects most of the material, which the female works into place. After the eggs hatch, the male builds a platform where he roosts and broods the young at night.

Tending the young *Both parents feed the young for about eight weeks.*

Nesting information March – September • 1 or 2 broods • 4–7 speckled, buff eggs • 21–24 days incubation: both sexes • 55–60 days fledging • Independent at fledging

---

Gull family *(Laridae)*

BLACK-HEADED GULL

Larus ridibundus

Length: 38 cm (15 in)

ALTHOUGH BASICALLY a seabird, the black-headed gull has moved inland this century, replacing the crow and kite as the urban scavenger. At first, black-headed gulls were winter visitors to towns and returned to the coast to breed. The species started to nest near to towns some time afterwards but inland breeding colonies have remained small. The inland gull roosts and nests in gravel pits, reservoirs and sewage works and commutes daily to feed on farmland and in city parks and gardens.

Dark spot on head

VOICE

There is a variety of harsh calls, including a repeated *kek* of alarm.

Young gull
Juveniles are a mottled, pale brown. By the time they are a year old, they have orange legs and beak, but retain some brown on the wings.

Red legs

Winter plumage
After the nesting season, the dark brown head-feathers disappear, except for marks behind the eyes.

FEEDING Black-headed gulls mainly eat insects and worms seized from the ground or stolen from other birds. They circle in upcurrents to catch flying ants and scavenge around dumps and waste ground.
Bird-table Gulls swoop down for scraps.

NESTING Black-headed gulls breed in colonies with nests close together. The simple nest of grass is built on the ground or, very exceptionally, on buildings.

Black head *A gull in summer breeding-dress carries food in its bulging crop (neck pouch).*

Nesting information *April – July • 1 brood • 3 brown-blotched, grey-green eggs • 23–26 days incubation: both sexes • 35 days fledging • 1 week until independent*

Pigeon family *(Columbidae)*

COLLARED DOVE

Streptopelia decaocto

Length: 32 cm (12½ in)

ALTHOUGH A COMMON bird over much of the country, the collared dove is a relative newcomer. Sixty years ago it started to spread westwards from its native home in south-eastern Europe. This tame and attractive bird reached Britain in the 1950s, and is now found over most of Europe. Perhaps because its new home is colder, the collared dove prefers to live in towns and villages, or near farms, where it can find plenty of food.

Black and white collar *(lacking in the juvenile)*

VOICE A repeated *coo-COO-coo* advertises the territory and is used in courtship. Although initially a gentle, pleasing sound, the monotonous cooing may become infuriating. Sometimes, when the collared dove gives only two *coos,* you may mistake it for the cuckoo. The dove gives a nasal *whurr-whurr* when excited, as in the male's display flight, which is similar to the woodpigeon's (p.44).

Pale grey and brown plumage

Elder *The purple berries are often eaten by collared doves.*

FEEDING The collared dove mainly eats seeds with some leaves, buds and fruit but occasionally feeds on caterpillars, snails and other small animals.
Bird-table It frequently feeds on grain, seeds, bread and scraps.

NESTING The female builds a flimsy platform of twigs in a tree, occasionally on a building, while the male gathers material. The nestlings are fed on *pigeon's milk* (p.45). Parents drive jays, magpies and even humans away from the nest.

Squabs – collared dove nestlings

Nesting information March – November • 3– 6 broods • 2 white eggs • 14–18 days
incubation: both sexes (female at night) • 17 days fledging • 1 week until independent

---

41

Pigeon family *(Columbidae)*

STREET PIGEON
Columba livia
Length: 33 cm (13 in)

Neck-patch
*The glossy lilac
and green is
typical of
the rock
dove.*

THIS FAMILIAR INHABITANT of towns and cities is a descendant of the rock dove that, centuries ago, was domesticated and selectively bred in dovecotes. The rock dove was kept for the table, for carrying messages or for racing in competitions. Street (or feral) pigeons are the wild descendants of a variety of domestic breeds and their numbers are continually being increased by domestic pigeons, still bred for show and racing, that have escaped from captivity or become lost on homing flights.

Plumage
*Pigeons are
usually grey-
blue, marked
with white –
often on
the rump
(p.130).*

Sunbathing *A domestic pigeon basks on the warm ground during summer sunshine. Although the street pigeon population is self-supporting, numbers are increased by a variety of breeds of domestic pigeon returning to the wild.*

VOICE The low, cooing *ooor-ooor* or *o-roo-coo* is a familiar sound in cities.

Living on the streets Street pigeons make friends by becoming hand-tame in parks and squares, but they are a problem for municipal authorities because they foul buildings and may spread disease. Despite attempts by authorities to restrict numbers, the bonanza of easily procured food in towns lets the pigeon population build up and allows many sick and injured pigeons to survive much longer than they would in natural conditions. As a result, you often see street pigeons with deformed legs or damaged bills.

Grounded *A racing pigeon takes its bearings before flying to its home loft. Racing breeds have a remarkable homing ability; competitors enter them in races of up to 500 miles long.*

Flight *Strong breast-muscles and a heavy body make pigeons powerful fliers.*

FEEDING Street pigeons eat any spilt grain, seeds, bread and other edible litter. At one time grain from horses' nosebags was an important food but nowadays litter from fast-food outlets provides a ready supply. Many urban pigeons take at least some of their food from handouts in squares and parks. Some pigeons even learn to recognize individuals who provide food regularly and will approach these people when they appear.
Bird-table Grain, bread and kitchen scraps.

Cultivated grain

Fan-shaped tail *The garden fantail, seen feeding on seeds under the bird-table, is a variety of pigeon that breeds well in dovecotes.*

NESTING The nest of twigs is built by the female, with the assistance of the male, on a ledge or in a hole. Pairs may nest all year if conditions are favourable. As with other members of the pigeon family, nestlings are only given solid food after a period of 10 days (p.45).
Nest-box Enclosed nest-box (p.115). Dovecotes – wooden "houses" separated into compartments – are also used, both for roosting and nesting.

Brooding *A street pigeon settles down on the nest and covers a squab (a young pigeon) to protect it and keep it warm.*

Nesting information *Mainly March – September • 2 or 3 broods • 2 white eggs • 17–18 days incubation: both sexes • 49 days fledging • 1 week until independent*

Pigeon family *(Columbidae)*

WOODPIGEON

Columba palumbus
Length: 40 cm (16 in)

White and green neck-patch
(The juvenile lacks this patch and is duller overall.)

I N THE COUNTRYSIDE, farmers regard the woodpigeon as a pest because of its appetite for cereals, root crops and legumes. Normally wary as a result, this large pigeon becomes tame in built-up areas, where you may see it walking towards a supply of food or water with a typically "pigeon-toed" gait. The male often advertises his presence in the territory, which may be no more than a single tree, simply by sitting conspicuously: a woodpigeon in a bare tree is difficult to miss.

Wing-flash A striking, white wing-flash separates the black outer wing and grey inner wing – most noticeable when in flight.

VOICE The song is a plaintive c*oo COO coo coo-coo,* the first faint note of which is easily missed. A bout of cooing ends with a final *cook.* You may hear a softer cooing during courtship, when the male bows before the female with his plumage puffed out and tail fanned.

Take-off When flying off, the woodpigeon's wings meet over its back with a sharp clap. The man-oeuvre is so strenuous that it will not be repeated in a hurry. Once disturbed, the bird settles in a tree, from which it can effortlessly launch itself by dropping.

Wing-claps

Glide

Black-tipped tail

Display flight You will see the display flight, which is a steep climb and glide, mostly in February and March (some time after the males take up territories in winter). At the top of the arc, one or two loud wing-claps can be heard. These are whipcracks on the down-stroke rather than the wings striking together.

Beak *The slightly hooked* ———— *beak – not found on other European pigeons – is designed for tearing leaves.*

FEEDING The woodpigeon likes legumes, especially peas and beans, and brassicas, such as cabbages, swedes, turnips and brussels sprouts. Other foods are acorns, beech mast, haws, elders and weed seeds, as well as worms, snails and insects. Do not be surprised to see a pigeon eating grit – it is used to grind food in its *gizzard* (the muscular part of the stomach).

Bird-table A rare visitor, the woodpigeon may come to ground stations for bread, seeds and vegetable scraps. It is more likely to visit for a drink at a garden pond or bird-bath.

Ivy food *In winter, look for woodpigeons eating ivy berries.*

Beech mast – *a favoured food*

Beak used as drinking-straw

Simple bird-bath (p.109)

Unique drinking *Pigeons put their beaks into water and suck; other birds raise their heads to let water trickle down their throats.*

Garden pest *Woodpigeons do serious damage to sprouts and cabbages in winter.*

NESTING Both parents assemble a flimsy platform, usually in a tree but sometimes on a building, from twigs gathered from the ground or snapped off trees. Eggs (laid at one- to three-day intervals) can be seen through the floor of the nest. If the nest is re-used, it becomes bulkier. The long nesting season is a result of the woodpigeon's ability to feed its *squabs* (nestlings) on *pigeon's milk* – a cheesy secretion from the crop, rich in protein and fat. Most other garden birds feed their young on insects, which are only available over a limited season.

Nesting information *February – November • 2 broods • 2 white eggs • 17 days incubation: both sexes • 20–35 days fledging • 1 week until independent*

Owl family *(Strigidae)*

TAWNY OWL
Strix aluco
Length: 38 cm (15 in)

M ORE OFTEN HEARD than seen because of its nocturnal lifestyle, the tawny owl is the most common hunting bird in gardens, preying mainly on small mammals (such as moles) and birds but also catching fish, amphibians, reptiles, worms, beetles and moths. Although it is rare to see a tawny owl by day, do keep a watch as it likes to sunbathe from time to time. Essentially a bird of mature woodlands, the tawny owl has been able to adapt even to city life where there are enough large trees, which are needed for roosting-places as well as nest sites.

VOICE The song is a hollow *hooo* followed by a wavering *hoo-hoo-hoo-ooooo*. A sharp *ke-wick* call is used by a pair to keep in contact. Listen for young owls repeatedly calling with a hissing *ke-sip* throughout summer nights.

Behaviour When alarmed, the tawny owl makes its body as slender as possible (here, it turns its head almost full circle to keep an eye on the threat). In contrast, in an aggressive posture, the owl widens its eyes and fluffs out its feathers to make itself appear larger.

Recognition
A tawny owl, with its unmistakable silhouette, is only likely to be confused with the much smaller little owl (p.48).

Alarm posture
Body is slender.

Aggressive posture
Owl widens body.

FEEDING Tawny owls in country gardens mainly catch mice and voles but town owls, like kestrels, chiefly feed on birds, up to the size of pigeons and mallards. Garden birds are killed mostly at dawn or dusk when they are just active but tawny owls have also been seen taking birds from their roosts. They also attack nests, dragging away the sitting adult and stealing the contents. Birds are plucked first and any prey that is initially too large to swallow is carried to a perch

Ambush
A tawny owl watches from a perch, then swoops down on prey.

Silencers
The fluffy fringes of flight-feathers deaden the sound of wing beats

and dismembered. Remains from plucking and pellets regurgitated after a meal accumulate on the ground, allowing the owl's diet to be studied. Although owls have good eyesight, prey is detected mainly by ear. Consequently rain and wind hamper hunting, although earthworms are easier to find on damp, warm nights when they come to the surface to feed and mate. The owl lands, listens intently then hops over the ground to seize the worm. Bad weather may force tawny owls to feed on carrion, such as animals killed on roads.

NESTING The tawny owl lays its eggs in a hole in a tree or building, or finds an abandoned squirrel or magpie nest. The eggs hatch at three- to four-day intervals. The young remain in the parents' territory and are fed by them until driven away when about three months old.
Nest-box Tawny owls will use a specially designed nest-box (p.113), particularly if natural sites are scarce.

Owlet *A fledgling tawny owl, with its distinctively barred, downy plumage, tries out its wings.*

Bird-table Tawny owls swoop down on bird-tables chiefly to catch small birds feeding there. The rare instances of tawny owls coming to feed on meat and fat are usually the result of severe weather.

Owl pellets *If you come across dried pellets (regurgitated, indigestible fur and bones) on the ground, look up and you may discover a tawny owl's roost.*

Nesting information *March – June • 1 brood • 3 or 4 white eggs • 28–30 days incubation: female • 32–37 days fledging • 12 weeks until independent*

Owl family *(Strigidae)*

LITTLE OWL

Athene noctua
Length: 22 cm (8¹/₂ in)

Recognition
This small, grey-brown owl is only half the size of a tawny owl (pp.46–7).

PARKLAND WITH TREES, even in towns and cities, is a favourite habitat of the little owl, which may stray into gardens. It is more visible than the tawny owl as it often hunts by day, especially when there are nestlings to feed. You are most likely to see one when it is hunting from a perch on a tree or fence post.

VOICE The male's hoot is a plaintive *kiew-kiew*, which the female answers with a scream. The call is a *kee-oo*.

FEEDING The little owl drops from its perch to prey on earthworms and insects, such as beetles, as well as small mammals and birds, and sometimes runs after them. It also chases craneflies and other flying insects with a bounding flight that is unique among owls.

Meal *A little owl eats an earthworm.*

NESTING There is no proper nest; the eggs are laid in a hole in a tree or building, or even in a rabbit hole. The young owls, which are more uniformly grey, may leave the nest before they can fly to explore along branches or vegetation. Warning calls from their parents send them scuttling back to safety.
Nest-box A large enclosed nest-box, partitioned to make it dark (p.115).

Nest site *The dark hole of an oak tree is ideal.*

Nesting information *April – July • 1 brood • 3–5 white eggs • 27–28 days incubation: female • 30–35 days fledging • 4 weeks until independent*

Swift family *(Apodidae)*

SWIFT

Apus apus

Length: 16.5 cm (6½ in)

Slender wings

Uniformly dark plumage

N O OTHER BIRD spends as much time in the air as the swift. After nesting, it may not land again until it returns to its nest the next spring, after mating on the wing. On summer evenings, flocks gather and then circle skywards until lost to sight. They spend the night in a semi-slumber, drifting with the wind, and descend at dawn. Swifts have short legs and rarely perch preferring to cling on to walls.

VOICE A screaming *sree*; also a chirping at the nest.

High flier *Swifts will fly up over half a mile high to catch insects, such as aphids, beetles and flying ants, carried up in turbulent air.*

Short, forked tail

FEEDING Swifts mainly feed on small flying insects and spiders floating on gossamer. They gather over lakes to feed on swarming midges. In cold, wet spells, flying insects disappear, causing swifts to travel long distances to find food.

Recognition
The swift is distinguished from the swallow and martins by its short, forked tail and long, scythe-shaped wings.

NESTING The swift's nest is a shallow cup of grasses, leaves and feathers, collected in the air and cemented with saliva. You can locate the site in holes in walls and under eaves when a bird flies up to it and then swoops away, leaving the occupants screaming. Nestlings put on weight rapidly and, by becoming torpid, can survive for a long time without being fed or brooded.

White throat

Juvenile *The fledging period depends on the availability of food.*

Nest-box Swifts will nest in a special box (p.115), with an entrance hole underneath.

Nesting information *Late May – August • 1 brood • 2 or 3 white eggs • 20–22 days incubation: both sexes • 5–7 weeks fledging • Independent at fledging*

Woodpecker family *(Picidae)*

GREEN WOODPECKER

Picus viridis

Length: 32 cm (12¹/₂ in)

L ARGE SIZE and bold colours make the green woodpecker an exciting visitor but it is not a common garden bird. Its bill, which is weaker than that of other woodpeckers, is used for chiselling soft wood only. Green woodpeckers drill holes into lawns where there are ants' nests, and push their long tongues into the soil to eat the insects.

Juvenile The juvenile is speckled and barred. (The adult has a black face, red crown and yellow rump.)

Tip of the tongue
The tongue can be extended 10 cm (4 in) so its flat, sticky tip can reach insects living deep in holes and crevices.

VOICE Loud, laughing calls can be heard.

FEEDING Woodpeckers mainly eat ants but also prey on beetles, moths and flies.
Bird-table On rare occasions, green woodpeckers take fat and mealworms.

NESTING Green woodpeckers may nest in large gardens if they can find suitable trees in which to excavate holes. The nest has a depth of up to 50 cm (20 in), and an entrance 6 cm (2¹/₂ in) in diameter. It may be re-used in succeeding years, but starlings tend to take it over.
Nest-box Green woodpeckers may use large enclosed nest-boxes (p.115).

Nest hole A woodpecker takes two to three weeks to excavate its chamber. (Close-up, you can spot the male by the red in his moustache.)

Nesting information *April – July • 1 brood • 5–7 white eggs • 17–19 days incubation: both sexes (male at night) • 23–27 days fledging • 3–7 weeks until independent*

Woodpecker family *(Picidae)*

GREAT SPOTTED WOODPECKER

Dendrocopos major
Length: 23 cm (9 in)

Sharp bill

A MIXED BLESSING in gardens, the great spotted woodpecker is an interesting visitor but it raids nest-boxes to eat young birds inside. Like other woodpeckers, the great spotted woodpecker has a stiff tail and unusual arrangement of toes – two face forwards and two backwards. These help it climb up trees and provide a firm base when the bird chisels wood to excavate holes.

Recognition It is larger than the lesser spotted woodpecker and has white patches on its short wings and red under its tail. The male has a crimson nape.

VOICE The "song" is a rapid (20 times per second) drumming of the bill on a branch, which sounds like a snore (the note varies according to the size and type of branch). A loud *chick* is used as a contact call.

FEEDING A variety of insects is eaten, from wood-boring beetles to flies caught in the air. Vegetable food includes pine, larch and spruce seeds, the seeds of birch and other hardwood trees as well as nuts, fruit and fungi. In Europe, but rarely in Britain, this woodpecker punctures trunks to drink sap.
Bird-table Suet, oats or nuts, in a birdfeeder or wedged in crevices.

Drilling Holes are bored in tree trunks to extract insects.

Almonds – opened by woodpeckers

NESTING Both sexes excavate the nest chamber, usually 3–5 m (10–16 ft) above ground. The hole, which is about 30 cm (12 in) deep, 12 cm (4¾ in) in diameter and has an entrance of 6 cm (2½ in) wide, takes up to four weeks to complete. The same hole is used in successive years, unless it is usurped by starlings.
Nest-box Great spotted woodpeckers may use large enclosed boxes (p.115).

Nesting information April–July • 1 brood • 4–7 white eggs • 10–13 days incubation: both sexes (male at night) • 21 days fledging • 1 week until independent

51

Swallow family *(Hirundinidae)*

HOUSE MARTIN

Delichon urbica
Length: 12.5 cm (5 in)

VOICE There is a soft, twittering song and chirping contact notes between mates, and between parents and offspring.

Blue-black above

White underneath

*Steep climb
– to snap up insects*

I N THE DAYS before buildings provided support for its nests, the house martin occupied cliffs and rock outcrops, where colonies can still be seen. Nowadays it often builds under the eaves or on a window frame of a house. The householder who is tired of cleaning soiled windows should fix a "splashboard" over the window.

Recognition
The house martin has shorter tail-streamers than a swallow. The white rump is conspicuous in flight.

FEEDING House martins feed on flying insects, mainly flies and aphids, but they may pick prey from the ground. Typically, a house martin suddenly climbs steeply, snaps an insect, then glides down.

NESTING Soon after house martins have returned in spring they prospect for suitable nest sites. The cup-nest is built with pellets of mud from the edge of puddles or ponds and is lined with feathers and grasses collected in the air. When the nestlings are grown, you can see their heads appear at the entrance. Adults try to lure them from the nest by hovering in front of it and calling. Eventually an adult bird lands at the nest, the youngster emerges and flies away with it. Later, you can see the fledglings meeting their parents in the air to receive food.
Nest-box Place bowl-nests (p.114) underneath the eaves for house martins.

Invitation to fly An adult house martin, which is not necessarily a parent, beckons to the nestlings as it flies past, tempting them to leave the safety of the nest for the first time.

Nesting information *Late May – September • 1 or 2 broods • 2–5 white eggs • 15 days incubation: both sexes • 22–32 days fledging • Time until independent unknown*

Swallow family *(Hirundinidae)*

SWALLOW
Hirundo rustica
Length: 19 cm (7½ in)

W HEN THE SWALLOW, the traditional herald of spring, arrives, you are most likely to see it over lakes and reservoirs, where there is an abundant supply of early insects. Occasionally there are reports of swallows remaining behind to winter in Europe rather than migrating back to Africa.

Distinctive russet throat and forehead

FEMALE

VOICE The song is a pleasant, rather quiet twittering. The contact call is a repeated *swit-swit-swit*.

Recognition
Long tail-streamers and more pointed wings distinguish the adult swallow from its close relatives, the sand and house martins.

FEEDING The swallow forages for insects in the air, either swooping low or circling overhead in graceful movements that are punctuated by swift, jinking turns. The long tail-feathers provide great flight manoeuvrability, making the swallow more efficient at catching prey than swifts or martins. If flying insects are scarce, the swallow may take insects from leaves or the ground. Bluebottle-sized flies are preferred but butterflies, moths and other large insects are also caught. Greenfly and other tiny insects are hunted by swallows in cold weather.

NESTING The beams and ledges of buildings have almost replaced cliff-side ledges as sites for the saucer of mud and grass (p.155). (During a dry spell in the garden, water a patch of soil to provide mud.) The male circles above his chosen site, singing to attract a female. Sometimes eggs are laid in a neighbour's nest.
Nest-box Make a bowl-nest (p.114).

Feeding the young The nestlings are fed with balls of insects from their parents' throats.

Nesting information May – August • 2 or 3 broods • 4 or 5 red-spotted, white eggs • 14–15 days incubation: female • 19–21 days fledging • Several weeks until independent

Pipit family *(Motacillidae)*

PIED WAGTAIL

Motacilla alba

Length: 18 cm (7 in)

Recognition *Wagtails have bold black and white plumage, but in winter, the black throat turns white.*

ALTHOUGH ESSENTIALLY a waterside bird, the pied wagtail has adapted to man-made habitats. You can see it feeding in gardens, parks, on top of houses or picking its way over rubbish tips. The best time for watching wagtails is when they come on to lawns to gather small insects for their offspring. The long tail gives the wagtail superb manoeuvrability as it runs across the grass to lunge at prey or springs up to snap winged insects.

Tail *When standing still, wagtails continually bob their long tails. Why they do this is a mystery.*

VOICE The pied wagtail gives a loud, sharp *chissick* in flight and also sounds a musical *chee-wee* in defence of territory.

FEEDING Pied wagtails feed on small insects, especially flies, and other animals, such as small snails and earthworms, and they occasionally eat small seeds.

Bird-table Stale crumbs are taken from the ground, especially in hard weather.

Hunt *Look out for a pied wagtail (right) scurrying across the lawn when hunting.*

NESTING The cup-nest of grass, roots and mosses is built in a hole in walls, buildings, piles of brushwood or old nests of larger birds. You may identify a female as her tail becomes bent from incubating.

Nest-box Place a bird-shelf (p.114) among ivy or other thick vegetation.

Out of the nest *A parent feeds a fledgling. The juvenile's tail is much shorter.*

Nesting information *April – August • 2 broods • 3–5 brown-freckled, whitish eggs • 13 days incubation: mainly female • 14 days fledging • 1 week until independent*

Wren family *(Troglodytidae)*

WREN

Troglodytes troglodytes
Length: 9.5 cm (3³/₄ in)

T HE ONLY EUROPEAN member of its family, the tiny, reddish-brown wren often appears mouse-like as it scurries along the edges of walls and borders and through undergrowth. Because the wren feeds on the ground, its food is cut off by ice and snow, and the population drops in a bad winter. Put up "umbrellas" of cut conifer branches to provide snow-free patches if there are no shrubs or hedges

Forceps-like beak

VOICE A loud, shrill trilling is sung all year round, except in late summer and early autumn. Calls include a hard *tick-tick-tick* and a rolling *churr.*

Tell-tale Look for the characteristic short, cocked tail.

FEEDING As well as tiny aphids plucked off leaves with their forceps-like beaks, wrens snatch caterpillars, grubs and spiders. Amazingly, wrens have been known to steal small goldfish from ponds.

NESTING The male constructs several nests in holes in walls, banks and trees or in old nests of other birds. The nest is a globe of dead leaves, grass and moss with a side entrance (p.155). The male sings near a nest to entice a female to it. If she accepts, she adds a lining of feathers and lays the eggs. When food is abundant, a male may persuade two or more females to lay in his territory.
Nest-box Wrens nest in open-fronted boxes (p.115) and, occasionally, tit-boxes (p.110) and may use either of them for winter roosting. (Sometimes several wrens roost together to conserve heat.)

Bird-table Although a rare visitor, the wren takes tiny pieces of cake and breadcrumbs, especially from the ground. Sprinkle grated cheese among leaf litter as a special treat.

Hidden nest A wren feeds its young at a nest in a wall, concealed behind tangled foliage.

Nesting information Late April – July • 2 broods • 5 or 6 usually white eggs • 14–15 days incubation: female • 16–17 days fledging • 1–3 weeks until independent

Accentor family *(Prunellidae)*

DUNNOCK
Prunella modularis
Length: 14.5 cm (5³/₄ in)

Recognition
The adult has a grey head, throat and breast. (Juveniles are more striped.)

Y OU MIGHT OVERLOOK the dunnock (once known as the hedge sparrow) because its plumage is rather like the house sparrow's. However, the dunnock's shy, skulking habits, which keep it near cover, are very different. You may see the male flick both wings in courtship or give an aggressive display by quivering one wing.

Thin bill *Compare with sparrows'.*

Ground-feeder
A dunnock feeds beneath a bird-table.

VOICE The song – warbling phrases, lasting four to five seconds – is similar to a wren's, only less powerful. The male has a repertoire of phrases copied from nearby dunnocks. The year-round song reaches a peak in March. A shrill *tseep* keeps a pair in touch.

FEEDING The diet is almost entirely seeds in winter and mainly sluggish insects in summer. The dunnock picks beetles, spiders, flies, caterpillars and bugs from plants or the ground.
Bird-table The dunnock sometimes comes to quiet bird-tables, but it feeds regularly on crumbs from the ground and occasionally on meat and seeds.

NESTING The nest of twigs and moss, lined with moss and hair, is built by the female in thick hedges, shrubs and evergreens. Dunnocks have a complex mating system (p.10), with males helping to feed the nestlings of each female with which they have mated.

Egg colour *Dunnocks are often foster parents to cuckoos. A cuckoo egg (right) contrasts with the dunnock's, but usually mimics other species' eggs.*

Nesting information *April – August • 2 or 3 broods • 4 or 5 blue eggs • 14 days incubation: female • 12 days fledging • 2 weeks until independent*

Warbler family *(Sylviidae)*

GOLDCREST
Regulus regulus
Length: 9 cm (3½ in)

THERE ARE RECORDS of the goldcrest, the smallest European bird, being trapped in spiders' webs. You may mistake goldcrests for tits, whose flocks they often join, as they search among foliage for insects and spiders. Once you have learnt the goldcrest's distinctive song and call notes, you will immediately recognize its presence in your garden.

VOICE The song is a thin, twittering *tweedly-tweedly-tweedly-twiddledidee*; the call is a thin *see-see*.

Short, needle-thin bill – *for picking up the tiniest of insects*

Olive-green *above*

Characteristic crest
The crest is yellow, bordered with black. Males display by spreading their crests, which are partly orange. (Juveniles lack the coloured crest.)

Wing-bars
There are two pale-coloured stripes on each wing.

FEEDING The goldcrest eats many kinds of spiders and insects, especially flies, aphids and beetles, and their larvae, but it occasionally takes larger types of insects, such as adult moths.
Bird-table Crumbs, fat and grated cheese are eaten, especially in bad weather.

Shelter *By hunting under the dense foliage of evergreens, goldcrests can continue to find food even after a heavy snowfall.*

NESTING Planting cypress, larch or other conifers will encourage goldcrests to nest, but they also use ivy and gorse. At the start of the breeding season, the males display by spreading their crests. You can easily overlook the goldcrest, not so much because of its small size but because it lives among leaves. The nest, mostly built by the female, is slung underneath foliage near the end of a branch. It is made of moss and lichen, held together and suspended with spiders' webs (p.155).

Nesting information *April – July • 2 broods • 7–10 brown-spotted, white or buff eggs • 14–17 days incubation: female • 16–21 days fledging • Time until independent unknown*

Flycatcher family *(Muscicapidae)*

SPOTTED FLYCATCHER

Muscicapa striata
Length: 14 cm (5¹/₂ in)

A SUMMER VISITOR, the spotted flycatcher is instantly recognizable by its feeding behaviour. It lives almost exclusively on flying insects, which it chases with an erratic, jinking flight from a large circuit of perches. Its need for winged insects restricts the spotted flycatcher's stay in Europe to the summer. If the weather is unseasonably cold or wet, flycatchers may have to rely on insects plucked off leaves or the ground.

Plumage Light brown, streaked plumage sometimes appears almost grey. (Only juveniles are spotted.)

VOICE Although usually unnoticed, the quiet song is a collection of squeaky notes. The call of a spotted flycatcher is a thin *see*.

Aerial pursuit
A flycatcher flits out to snap up an insect before returning to its perch.

FEEDING The spotted flycatcher usually feeds on flies, but also bees, butterflies and greenfly. Once a flycatcher has collected the insects in one area, it has to move to a new perch. After a period of time, it can return for more forays from the original perch.

NESTING Nesting starts after other insect-eaters, such as warblers and tits. The young are fledged at the height of summer when hot days make for active insect life. The nest of moss, grass and twigs, bound by cobwebs and lined with hair and feathers, (p.154) is built mainly by the female, usually against a tree trunk or wall. An old nest may be used as a base.
Nest-box The flycatcher will use a bird-shelf (p.114) with a close perch.

Feeding the young A flycatcher brings a small tortoiseshell butterfly to its nestlings.

Nesting information May – June • 1 or 2 broods • 4 or 5 brown-spotted, greenish eggs •
12–14 days incubation: both sexes • 12–13 days fledging • 2–3 weeks until independent

---

Thrush family *(Turdidae)*

FIELDFARE

Turdus pilaris
Length: 25 cm (10 in)

Recognition
The fieldfare is a large thrush distinguished by its grey head and rump and chestnut back.

I N WINTER, LOUD, chuckling calls will alert you to the sight of a ragged flock of large thrushes flying past. These are fieldfares, as much the heralds of winter as swallows are of summer. A cold spell and a fall of snow sets flocks in motion – this is the time that you are most likely to see fieldfares in your garden, together with redwings (p.176).

White underwings
(These flash in flight.)

VOICE The song is a medley of chuckles and whistles interspersed with *chacks*. The call is a harsh *chack-chack-chack*.

FEEDING The main fieldfare food is earthworms, snails and other small animals. Fruit is eaten in winter, especially when animal food is unavailable. Crops of berries, such as hawthorn, holly and rowan, and windfall apples are particular attractions. A single fieldfare will try to defend a tree against all comers.
Bird-table Fieldfares are keen on old, rotten fruit left out on the ground.

NESTING The fieldfare breeds in northern, central and eastern Europe, with only a few pairs nesting in northern Britain. The nest is a cup of grasses, twigs and mud, lined with fine grasses, built in a tree but sometimes on the ground. The nest is often exposed, but several pairs of birds build near each other and are aggressive towards intruders. People, cats and magpies coming too close are "dive-bombed" with angry cries and are sometimes spattered with droppings.

Winter fruit *If an apple is past its prime, store it somewhere dark. Come winter, fieldfares will be grateful for it.*

Rowan berries
– fieldfare food

Nesting information April – May • 1 or 2 broods • 4–6 red-speckled, pale blue eggs •
13–14 days incubation: female • 14 days fledging • 2 weeks until independent

Thrush family *(Turdidae)*

ROBIN
Erithacus rubecula
Length: 14 cm (5¹/₂ in)

VOTED BRITAIN'S NATIONAL bird, the robin has spread into British gardens in a way that has not happened in the rest of Europe. Its natural habitat of woodland with a layer of undergrowth is mimicked by the hedges and shrubberies of British gardens. The roost is usually in dense vegetation, such as ivy, or in buildings and nest-boxes. Outside the breeding season, some robins join communal roosts.

Brown upper-parts and tail

Orange-red breast *(absent in juveniles, which are spotted)*

Nightlife
The robin's large eyes seem to have good night vision because you often see or hear a robin in the garden when it is so dark that you can only recognize it by its plump outline.

Robin at night

Territory Robins keep territories all year except during the moult period and the severest winter weather. Females usually defend their own separate territories in winter. A territory is needed not only for breeding but also to ensure a private food supply. Any robin without one will die within a few weeks, so defence of the territory is extremely aggressive. Usually the territory-owner only has to fluff out its red breast-feathers before the intruder retreats but rivals may come to blows and a fatal outcome is surprisingly common. If the thought of this is distressing, put out plenty of food, especially in hard weather.

VOICE You will hear bursts of liquid warbling all year. Both sexes sing to defend territory in winter. The male's more powerful spring song starts as early as December. Each robin may have several hundred different phrases. Alarm calls are a repeated *tic* and a thin *tseeee*.

Proclaiming territory
A robin declares its territory with a song.

FEEDING The robin mainly eats ground-living invertebrates – insects (especially beetles), snails, worms and spiders – but on rare occasions takes fish and tadpoles. From autumn to early spring, fruit and berries are an important part of the diet. Its chief method of hunting is well suited to the garden mixture of thick vegetation and open ground. The robin watches from a low perch, then drops down, seizes an

Catch and carry A robin brings insects to its young.

Winter food A robin appreciates a bowl of bread and cake crumbs in cold weather.

insect and flies up again. It also hops across the ground, pausing at intervals to watch for any moving prey. In their original habitat, robins followed pheasants, deer, wild boar and other large animals for any prey they disturbed. This is probably why robins in the garden are so trusting – they follow the gardener's spade as if it were the hoofs of a large mammal. Robins have even been known to follow moles working underground to catch worms escaping to the surface.

Bird-table Although mealworms are a great treat, robins eat any scraps of bread, meat, potatoes and fat. Some individuals take peanuts from hanging nets.

NESTING Robins pair up from December; usually the female joins the male on his territory. Pairing and nesting are earlier if the robins are well fed (bird-feeders help here). A hair-lined nest of moss and leaves, based on a pad of dead leaves, is built in a crevice in trees or in man-made objects, such as tins and letter-boxes. The male feeds the first family when the female lays another clutch.

Nest-box Open-fronted boxes (p.115), or sometimes tit-boxes with large holes.

Spring sight Young robins wait for food.

Nesting information April – July • 2 broods • 5 or 6 red-speckled, white or bluish eggs • 14 days incubation: female • 13–14 days fledging • 3 weeks until independent

Thrush family *(Turdidae)*

BLACKBIRD

Turdus merula

Length: 25 cm (10 in)

ALTHOUGH ORIGINALLY a bird of woodlands, the blackbird has become a successful garden bird because of its wide diet. The glossy, black male, with his bright yellow bill and eye-ring, is a familiar figure in the garden but the colours of the female and young birds may cause some confusion. By learning to identify the sex and age of blackbirds, you can make more sense of events in the garden. Pair-formation may start in the autumn before the nesting season, and you will often see territorial disputes, in which birds chase and attempt to fly up above one another.

ADULT MALE

Familiar glossy, black plumage

Juvenile male A young male (left) gorges himself on cotoneaster berries. The juvenile male has a dull plumage (with a brownish hue, especially on the wings), a dark bill and no eye-ring until his first winter.

VOICE The song consists of a couple of two-second phrases, often ending in a chuckle and sometimes interspersed with snatches of other birdsong as well as human whistles. You are most likely to hear the song of young males setting up their territories in February. It decreases after the eggs have been laid. A quiet subsong is heard in autumn. Several calls are heard for different situations, ranging from a subdued *pook-pook* when uneasy to a hysterical rattling when put to flight.

Aggressive display A blackbird threatens intruders away from its half-eaten apple with an aggressive open-beak display.

White bird
Blackbirds some-times have a few white feathers.

Pale eye-ring

Dark bill

Adult female *The female is dark brown, paler under-neath, with faint spots and streaks.*

FEEDING Fruit and berries (including cotoneaster, honeysuckle and barberry) are eaten in the latter half of the year, while earthworms, insects and other small animals are taken in spring and autumn. Caterpillars are an important food in summer but, as these are often rare in gardens, young are fed more on worms and adult insects. When hunting on a lawn, a blackbird cocks its head to one side before hopping forward to seize a worm from its burrow. It is not known whether the head posture helps the bird listen or look for earthworms (the latter is believed to be more likely). Blackbirds catch tadpoles and fish from ponds and steal food from other birds, such as large snails from song thrushes.

Bird-table Try putting out a variety of foods, including scraps, bread, fat, seeds and old fruit, such as apples and pears.

Rummaging for food When foraging (right), one foot is raked backwards through dead leaves or loose soil as the bill flicks for food.

NESTING The female builds a solid nest, usually in a shrub or hedge. Dry vegeta-tion, which the male may help her collect, is reinforced with mud. The male some-times stands guard over the eggs when the female is away feeding. The family is divided after fledging and each parent feeds particular youngsters, but the male may look after the whole family if the female has a new clutch to incubate.

Nest-box A large bird-shelf (p.114).

Leaf-lined nest A lining of dead leaves or, usually, fine grasses distinguishes the black-bird's nest from that of the song thrush (p.65).

Nesting information *March – June • 3–5 broods • 3–5 brown-freckled, greenish-blue eggs • 13 days incubation: female • 13–14 days fledging • 3 weeks until independent*

Thrush family *(Turdidae)*
SONG THRUSH
Turdus philomelos
Length: 23 cm (9 in)

Recognition
*The song
thrush is
a warmer
brown than
the mistle
thrush.*

A REGULAR GARDEN VISITOR, the song thrush is more often seen feeding on the lawn and in flowerbeds than at the bird-table. It is one of the best garden songsters and its far-carrying whistling, unlike the blackbird's song, can be heard almost all year round. Its loud contribution to the dawn chorus that you hear on mild winter mornings is linked to the defence of territories. In cold weather, or if food is otherwise in short supply, song thrushes living in the countryside may join those already in gardens.

VOICE The song is composed of clear, fluting phrases, usually repeated three or four times, and delivered from a tree-top perch. A call note *tick* is given in flight and there are blackbird-like notes of alarm (p.62). As summer advances, you may hear fledged young calling to their parents with sharp *chicks* from their hideouts in the undergrowth.

Wings The orange flash beneath each wing distinguishes the song thrush from the mistle thrush (p.66) and fieldfare. The red-wing has an even more obvious flash.

**Tree-top
perch**

FEEDING The song thrush feeds on insects and other invertebrates. Worms are an important food, especially in the earlier part of the year, as is fruit (including fallen apples, and elder, holly and rowan berries) in autumn. Snails are an emergency ration, mostly taken in winter frosts or summer droughts when hard ground makes worms difficult to come by. To break open the snails' protective shells, song thrushes dash them against a hard "anvil", such as a stone, path or tree root. Breaking shells and sorting through the

Distinctive feeding method The song thrush hops or runs forward, occasionally pauses to look for prey (with its head cocked to one side) and then pounces, often on an earthworm.

Yew berries *Song thrushes eat the red, fleshy fruits without digesting the poisonous seeds.*

untidy remains is a laborious and time-consuming task that is not worthwhile when other food is readily available. Only song thrushes smash open snails but watch for blackbirds waiting to snatch the snail flesh from them.

Bird-table Shyness often keeps the song thrush from the bird-table but it does feed underneath, taking fat, sultanas and kitchen scraps. It appreciates apples left in quiet corners, near to the cover offered by hedges and shrubs.

Snail smashing *A tapping noise may reveal the presence of a song thrush in the garden. To get at the soft flesh, the thrush grips the lip of the snail's shell and batters it against an anvil.*

Snail remains
Broken shells litter the anvil.

NESTING The female constructs the solid, cup-shaped nest from grasses, leaves, roots and twigs embedded in earth. The smooth nest lining, of dung or mud mixed with saliva, is a trademark of the song thrush. A well-shaded site is usually chosen for the nest: low in a bush, tree or among the thick foliage of creepers, such as ivy. The same nest may be re-used for further broods.

Mud-lined nest *The smooth mud lining that stiffens the song thrush's bulky nest may sometimes be missing in dry summers.*

Nesting information *March–August • 2 or 3 broods • 4–6 black-spotted, blue eggs • 13–14 days incubation: female • 26–28 days fledging • 3 weeks until independent*

65

Thrush family *(Turdidae)*

MISTLE THRUSH
Turdus viscivorus
Length: 27 cm (10¹/₂ in)

VOICE Song is a far-carrying, ringing variation of *tee-tor-tee-tor-tee*. A harsh, rattling call is given when alarmed.

THE LARGEST EUROPEAN thrush, the aggressive mistle thrush requires a large territory so it is never abundant. It is so named because it feeds on mistletoe. In Great Britain, where mistletoe is less common, the species used to be known as the holly thrush because of its fondness for the deep red berries of holly bushes.

Recognition
Larger than the song thrush, the mistle thrush has greyer plumage.

FEEDING A wide range of insects and fruit is eaten. In early winter, the loose flocks break up and mistle thrushes defend territories around crops of mistletoe, yew, hawthorn or holly from other birds.
Bird-table Kitchen scraps, bread and apples. Mistle thrushes may defend a bird-table supply from other visitors.

Take-off *Pale underwings contrast with the song thrush's flash (p.64).*

Holly berries

NESTING The female takes one to two weeks to build a grass-lined nest of earth and plants, usually in a fork of a tree. Cats, birds of prey and people that come too close to the nest are attacked. Once fledged, the juveniles form small flocks.

Two broods *Although both adult birds feed the nestlings initially, the male continues to feed the first brood on his own once the female lays her second clutch.*

Nesting information   *Late February – July • 2 broods • 4 speckled, whitish eggs • 12–15 days incubation: female • 12–15 days fledging • 2 weeks until independent*

Long-tailed tit family *(Aegithalidae)*

LONG-TAILED TIT

Aegithalos caudatus
Length: 14 cm (5¹/₂ in)

*Recognition   The plumage is mainly
black and white. (Juveniles
are browner.)*

Long tail

VOICE
There is no proper
song, but a sharp
tsirrup and thin,
repeated *zee* are given
in flight and a short
pit when perched.

YOU ARE MOST likely to see parties of
long-tailed tits passing through the
garden rather than visiting a bird-
table. The flocks mainly comprise
parents and their offspring of
the year. Apart from helping
each other to find food and avoid
predators, the flock members huddle
together on cold nights to keep warm.
In February or March, winter parties
disband and males set up their own
territories within the flock territory and
mate with females from other flocks.

Pinkish tinge on body

FEEDING   Long-tailed tits eat far fewer
seeds than other tits and mainly take
insects and other invertebrates. They are
agile in their search of leaves and twigs,
but, unlike other tits, do not hold food
under the foot while pecking at it.
Instead, they hang upside down by one
foot while clutching the food in the other.

NESTING   Nest-building starts in February
or March and takes about three weeks
because the nest is extremely elaborate.
The ball of moss, spiders' webs, hair,
feathers and lichen (p.155) is built by both
sexes in a bush, bramble thicket, hedge or
high in a fork of a tree. The nestlings are
sometimes fed by helpers. These are
close relatives who have lost their own
nests to predators.

*Feather lining   The hundreds of feathers that
are added to the nest make the lining so snug
that when the female is incubating she has to
fold her tail over her back to fit inside.*

Bird-table   Some long-tailed tits form the
habit of visiting, especially when ice locks
up natural food. They prefer small fragments of meat, fat and peanuts and
are tempted by fat smeared on
to the bark of trees.

Spider – a favoured natural food

Nesting information   *March – May • 1 brood • 8–12 reddish-freckled, white eggs •
14–18 days incubation: female • 15–16 days fledging • Independent at next nesting season*

Tit family *(Paridae)*

BLUE TIT

Parus caeruleus

Length: 11.5 cm (4¹/₂ in)

THE BLUE TIT is one of the most delightful birds to visit the birdfeeder because of its bold, perky behaviour and the skilful acrobatics it performs on nut bags and tit-bells. One of the most frequent users of the bird-table, the blue tit is credited with high intelligence, partly due to its habit of investigating new sources of food and using its dexterity of foot and beak to obtain them. Studies with ringed birds have shown that over 100 blue tits may visit a garden in succession, although only a few can be seen at one time. Not many travel more than six miles on their daily round, although some migrate over 60 miles from their summer breeding-grounds.

Recognition *You can tell a blue tit by the bright blue on its cap and wings. (Juveniles are generally duller and have yellow cheeks.)*

VOICE The blue tit song is *tsee-tsee-tsu-hu-hu-hu-hu*. Calls include a thin *tsee-tsee*, which is used to keep in contact, a harsh *tsee* and a *churr* of alarm.

Blue wings

Fast food *The content of your nut bag decreases rapidly if blue tits can pull out whole peanuts and carry them away to eat at leisure.*

Threat posture
In an aggressive display, a blue tit threatens other birds by raising the feathers on its head to make it look bigger.

Bright blue cap

White cheeks

Bright yellow underparts

Keeping clean *As well as being a frequent visitor to the bird-table, the blue tit also enjoys using a bird-bath.*

An apple a day
When blue tits feed
on windfall apples,
they are not only
interested in
eating the fruit's
flesh but will
tunnel through it
to reach the seeds.

Bird-table Peanuts, seeds, fruit, fat, meat and assorted scraps are eaten. The blue tit is one of the most agile garden birds and is fun to watch as it feeds on hanging baskets, tit-bells, suet sticks, halved coconuts or strings of peanuts.

NESTING Nest-building starts with the female chipping at the entrance of a hole or crevice (even if it is a suitably sized hole in a nest-box). The time taken to collect material and build the nest varies from a few days to several weeks, if work is held up by bad weather. The nest of moss, dried grasses and small twigs is lined with fine grasses and feathers.
Nest-box Blue tits are among the most frequent users of tit-boxes (p.110).

Large clutch *One egg was laid each morning*
until this clutch of 10 eggs was complete.

FEEDING The diet comprises insects in summer and a mixture of insects and seeds, especially beech mast, in winter. Buds are stripped in search of small insects – aphids and weevils are often eaten but caterpillars provide the bulk of food needed for rearing the nestlings. Blue tits sometimes visit willow catkins and the flowers of gooseberries, currants and other garden plants for nectar. A natural resourcefulness enables blue tits to take advantage of changing crops, while their tameness allows them to exploit food deliberately or unwittingly left out. Once a feeding method has been adapted to suit a new food, blue tits quickly learn from each other, as happened with their habit of stealing milk (p.126).

Seeds (right) – *one of*
the many foods that
attract blue tits

Table-talk *Blue tits*
(left) *squabble over their*
shares of a bird pudding.

Nesting information *March – June* • *1 or 2 broods* • *5–12 reddish-flecked, white*
eggs • *14 days incubation: female* • *18 days fledging* • *4 weeks until independent*

Tit family *(Paridae)*

GREAT TIT
Parus major
Length: 14 cm (5 1/2 in)

Greyish-blue and green upperparts

Due to its readiness to use a nest-box, the great tit is one of the best studied of all birds. By saturating an area with nest-boxes almost the entire population of great tits can be persuaded to nest, allowing the progress of their breeding to be monitored easily. Natural nest holes in trees are scarcer in gardens than woods, so tit-boxes have a strong chance of being used by some of the great tits that have regularly attended the birdfeeders in your garden through the winter.

Recognition *You can recognize the great tit by its size – it is the largest member of the tit family.*

Gender gap *You can easily distinguish the female by her narrower black breast-stripe and less glossy plumage. Noticing the difference shows you that males dominate at feeders.*

VOICE In late winter, depending on the mildness of the weather, great tits start associating in pairs and become more vocal. A male sings most intensely to acquire a mate but, until the young have flown, he will also sing to advertise his territory. Great tits have one of the largest vocal repertoires of any small bird. Each tit's song incorporates several different phrases, which are variations on a basic phrase, described as *teacher-teacher* or a squeaky bicycle pump. With practice, it is possible to differentiate between individuals. Perhaps not surprisingly, the tits also recognize each other's songs and do not react to the familiar song of a neighbour, whose presence next to their territory they have come to

Black and white head

Bright yellow belly

Broad breast-stripe

Dominant male *The male whose territory encompasses the bird-table will chivvy visiting great tits – they are allowed on to the birdfeeder as long as they know their place and do not attempt to assert themselves.*

Calls Great tits have a range of calls: birdwatchers say that if you cannot identify the call of a garden bird, it is sure to be a great tit!

accept. However, territory-owners will respond immediately to a stranger's song because it represents a dangerous intrusion into their property.

There is an amazing variety of calls: the great tit's most familiar *pink* call is given by territory-holders and a churring note is given when disturbed. In late summer, the sibilant *tsee-tsee-tsee* calls give away the presence of youngsters that have only recently left the nest.

Insect hunt
A great tit climbs up a tree to search and probe for insects.

Tail – used as support

Hazelnuts – enjoyed by great tits

FEEDING Winter food for great tits is largely tree seeds, such as beech mast and even hazelnuts. Great tits are not as agile as other tits and spend more time feeding on the ground. Summer food is mainly insects, especially weevils, but also spiders and small snails.

Bird-table Peanuts, seeds, meat bones and fat. Hanging peanut bags, scrap baskets or halved coconuts filled with bird pudding allow you the opportunity to observe the antics of great tits.

NESTING The female builds the nest of moss in the hollow or cleft of a tree, or in a hole in a wall, and lines it with hair. The amount of time during which the fledglings continue to be fed depends on whether or not there is another brood, although a second clutch is a rare event.

Nest-box Large and standard-sized tit-boxes (p.110). The great tit is one of the most common users of nest-boxes. ·

Delivering food A great tit returns to its nest hole with food (usually moth caterpillars) for its hungry young family.

Nesting information April – July • 1 or 2 broods • 5–12 reddish-spotted, white eggs • 13–14 days incubation: female • 18–20 days fledging • 1–2 weeks until independent

Pine

Tit family *(Paridae)*

COAL TIT

Parus ater

Length: 11 cm (4¹/₄ in)

THE COAL TIT does not use bird-tables and nest-boxes as often as blue and great tits and is less likely to leave its woodland home in winter, only visiting suburbs if there is a food shortage. The coal tit is most at home among conifers – its long toes make it easy to grip bunches of conifer needles.

Black cap and white cheeks

Long toes

VOICE The song is *teachoo-teachoo* – similar to the great tit's song, but higher-pitched. The *tsee-tsee* call resembles that of a goldcrest.

Recognition Identify the coal tit by the white stripe on its nape (p.142).

FEEDING Using its slender beak, the coal tit probes crevices for tiny insects, or extracts seeds from cones in winter. Seeds, nuts and even insects are hoarded (p.125). A coal tit may empty a hopper of seeds, causing some plants to grow in odd places.

Bird-table Peanuts, seeds and fat.

Slender beak
The beak, longer than that of other tits, is better for carrying nuts.

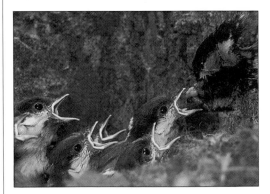

NESTING The nest is made in a hollow or cleft, usually low in a tree, or in a mouse-hole if no tree sites are available. The nest of moss is usually lined with hair, distinguishing it from the (usually feather-lined) nest of a blue tit (p.69).
Nest-box A coal tit will use a tit-box (p.110), especially if placed on a conifer.

Begging for food Fully feathered nestlings in a tree-hole nest gape to receive caterpillars.

Nesting information April – June • 1 or 2 broods • 7–12 reddish-spotted, white eggs •
17–18 days incubation: female • 16 days fledging • 2 weeks until independent

---

Nuthatch family *(Sittidae)*

NUTHATCH

Sitta europaea
Length: 14 cm (5½ in)

Awl-shaped beak

T HE NUTHATCH IS a woodland bird that visits gardens with mature trees. It usually feeds high in the canopy, where it gives away its presence by loud, cheerful calls, but it is a frequent visitor to the bird-table. In autumn and winter, nuthatches feed among flocks of tits.

VOICE The song is a rapid, trilling *chi-chi-chi*, heard mostly from January to May. The loud, ringing *chit-chit* call is heard all year round.

Recognition
The nuthatch has a streamlined body, short tail and black eye-stripe.

FEEDING The nuthatch probes crevices for spiders and insects. From autumn onwards, hazelnuts, acorns and beechnuts are wedged firmly into holes and hammered open by the powerful, awl-shaped beak, making a tapping noise that can be mistaken for a woodpecker chipping at the tree. Some nuts are stored in crevices.
  Bird-table Peanuts, sunflower seeds, cake and fat-smeared tree trunks.

Sign of a nuthatch
A hazelnut shell lies wedged in the bark of an oak tree, after having been opened.

Headfirst
Woodpeckers and treecreepers only move up trees, using their tails as props, but the nuthatch can hop down with equal skill.

NESTING Both sexes choose a hole in a tree or wall or take an abandoned nest. They plaster the entrance with mud or dung (probably to reduce the hole size and prevent larger birds taking over) and line the hollow with leaves or bark flakes.
Nest-box Enclosed nest-box (p.115).

Sealed Mud has been plastered on to a box.

Nesting information   Late April – June • 1 brood • 6–9 reddish-spotted, white eggs •
14–15 days incubation: female • 23–25 days fledging • Several days until independent

Treecreeper family *(Certhiidae)*

TREECREEPER

Certhia familiaris
Length: 12.5 cm (5 in)

Long, down-curved beak

GARDENS WITH MATURE trees will attract treecreepers, especially in winter. Unlike nuthatches and tits, which also search bark for food, treecreepers do not hang head-down and only hop upwards, using their strong tails as props like miniature woodpeckers. Inspect the trunks of dead trees: streaks of droppings mark roost sites (p.138).

VOICE The song is a thin, sibilant succession of notes ending in a little flourish: *see-see-see-sissi-sooee*, reminiscent of a loud goldcrest or high-pitched chaffinch. The repeated *see* and *sit* call notes are often thin and difficult to hear.

Fledgling (Adults have longer tails.)

Searching *The tree-creeper flies to a base of a tree, hunting for insects as it climbs up.*

FEEDING The diet is almost entirely small insects and spiders plucked from bark – rarely from foliage or the ground.
Bird-table Treecreepers may come to the bird-table but are more surely attracted if you smear a mixture of chopped nuts and porridge, or fat, over bark or into holes.

NESTING Both sexes build a nest from twigs, grasses and moss and line it with feathers. They place it behind a flap of bark or the cladding of a building, in a crevice or hollow, or occasionally in dense vegetation, such as ivy. Once fledged, family parties often join tits and goldcrests in mixed flocks.
Nest-box A specially designed, wedge-shaped box (p.112) is sometimes used if natural nest sites are scarce.

Chick-rearing An adult bird feeds a moth to its young. The nest is located behind some loose bark on a tree trunk.

Nesting information April – June • 1 or 2 broods • 5–7 brown-spotted, white eggs •
14–15 days incubation: female • *14–15 days fledging* • *Time until independent unknown*

Finch family *(Fringillidae)*
CHAFFINCH
Fringilla coelebs
Length: 15 cm (6 in)

T HE CHAFFINCH IS a woodland bird but it is also common in gardens and parks where tall trees provide food and song-posts. In good years, flocks of chaffinches gather under beech trees to feed on beech mast. Study the birds carefully to see if any of the closely related bramblings (which have orange bodies) are among them.

MALE

Conspicuous white flashes on wings and tail

VOICE The song is a regular series of repeated notes that ends with a flourish: *chip-chip-chip-chuwee-chuwee-tissichooee.* The call is a sharp *pink-pink.*

Plumage In spring, the cock chaffinch's buff feather tips wear away to reveal the brighter colours of the breeding plumage.

Breeding plumage – a colourful mixture of pink, chestnut and slate-blue

Female The hen resembles a female sparrow, but look for white on wings and tail.

FEEDING The chaffinch mainly eats seeds that have fallen on the ground, including beech mast, cereal grains, chickweeds and charlock. The parents feed the young on caterpillars, flies, spiders and other small animals.

Bird-table Chaffinches eat a variety of seeds and scraps, often picking up spillings under the bird-table rather than landing on it themselves.

NESTING The female builds a delicate nest, mostly of grass and moss, (p.154) in a tree fork. It is lined with feathers and rootlets and decorated on the outside with lichens and spiders' webs. The female takes over a thousand trips to gather the nest material. The male accompanies her as she works but does not help.

Patient fledgling
A fledgling chaffinch waits for food among flowering oak. During the breeding season, adult birds switch to collecting insects to feed their young.

Nesting information *May – August • 1 or 2 broods • 3–5 purple-marked, blue eggs • 12–14 days incubation: female • 12–14 days fledging • 2–3 weeks until independent*

Finch family *(Fringillidae)*

GOLDFINCH

Carduelis carduelis

Length: 12 cm (4³/₄ in)

THIS JEWEL OF a bird is less likely to visit a well-kept garden. The best way to attract goldfinches is to ensure a crop of seeding thistles, dandelions, groundsel or sowthistles, although they have also started to feed at peanut bags. A small flock of goldfinches energetically attacking seed heads is a delightful sight. If you see a goldfinch on teazel, it is likely to be male because the slightly duller female, whose bill is fractionally shorter, has difficulty extracting the seeds. Goldfinches may take the seeds of garden plants such as lavender.

Seed-head specialist
The slender bill is ideal for probing for seeds.

Bold patches of yellow and red

VOICE The call is a liquid *swit-witt-witt* and the song is a twittering, rambling variation on these notes.

FEEDING Large teazel, thistle and burdock seeds are preferred but when they run out the goldfinch eats the smaller groundsel, dandelion, ragwort or sowthistle seeds. It also eats the seeds of elm, birch and pine.
Bird-table Peanuts and cage-bird seeds, such as millet (p.105), are eaten.

Teazel
The seeds lie at the bottom of long tubes, surrounded by bristles.

Duller fledgling
The juvenile has a streaked, grey-brown body and is less colourful on the head. Buff feathers conceal the distinctive gold wing-bar.

NESTING The female builds a cup-nest of moss, roots and lichens, lined with wool and thistle-down, often near the end of a branch. The territories are small and several pairs of birds may nest close to each other. Courtship involves both sexes spreading their wings and tails to show off their colourful plumage.

Nesting information *April – August • 2 or 3 broods • 4–6 red-freckled, white eggs • 11–13 days incubation: female • 13–16 days fledging • 2 weeks until independent*

Finch family *(Fringillidae)*

GREENFINCH

Carduelis chloris
Length: 14.5 cm (5³/₄ in)

THE GREENFINCH HAS become more common in gardens as it gradually colonized towns and cities during this century. This is partly because of the loss of grain and weed seeds due to intensive farming, but the greenfinch has also changed habitat to exploit peanuts and sunflower seeds in feeders.

VOICE The male's rasping *sweee* betrays greenfinches hidden in foliage. The song is a medley of notes ending in a loud wheeze. A repeated *chi-chi-chi-chi* is given in flight.

Yellow wing-patches
These distinguish females from sparrows.

Recognition
Greenfinches have green and yellow plumage. The female is duller.

FEEDING The diet comprises a wide assortment of seeds, including elm, yew, bramble, dandelion and burdock.
Bird-table As well as feeding on peanuts and sunflower seeds in hoppers and hanging bags, greenfinches also gather on the ground underneath bird-tables or nearby perches to collect the seed fragments dropped by other birds.

NESTING Greenfinches, unlike most other birds, remain sociable through the breeding season. They nest in small colonies of about half a dozen pairs, usually in a dense shrub. The female builds the nest of twigs, grass and moss and lines it with hair and rootlets (p.154).

Mixed diet Nestlings stretch and gape as a parent returns. Caterpillars and aphids are important for nestlings, but the young receive only regurgitated seeds once they leave the nest.

Nesting information *April – August • 2 or 3 broods • 4 – 6 red-spotted, white eggs • 12 – 14 days incubation: female • 13 – 16 days fledging • 2 weeks until independent*

77

Finch family *(Fringillidae)*

SISKIN

Carduelis spinus

Length: 12 cm (4³/₄ in)

Grey-green plumage

A NEWCOMER TO GARDENS over the last 30 years, the siskin is a small finch with the acrobatic habits of a tit. It searches for food at the tips of slender twigs, where it hangs upside-down as it pecks at cones and bunches of seeds. The favourite foods of the siskin are the seeds of birch, alder and conifers. The siskin was probably first attracted to gardens by the planting of ornamental conifers, such as cypress. It is now a regular winter visitor and comes into gardens especially when natural seed crops are exhausted.

FEMALE

Yellow rump and sides of tail

Forked tail

Recognition *The female is greenish-yellow, with dark streaks beneath. The male (below) has a black cap and bib, is less streaked and generally brighter.*

Alder catkins and cones

VOICE The song is a twittering, ending in a wheeze. The calls are a *tsooee* and a twitter given on the wing.

Black cap

Yellow wing-bars

MALE

FEEDING Siskins take seeds from spruce and pine cones as well as alder, birch, elm, thistles and dock. Insects are fed to growing nestlings.

Bird-table Peanuts, fat and a variety of seeds. For some unknown reason, the siskin is particularly attracted to peanuts in red plastic mesh bags, or other red containers.

NESTING The female builds the tidy, compact nest from small, lichen-covered twigs and lines it with rootlets, hair and feathers. It is usually sited near the end of a branch, high off the ground in a conifer. Recent, widespread plantations of conifers throughout Europe have increased the species' range.

Nesting information *May – August • 2 broods • 3–5 red-streaked, pale blue eggs • 12 days incubation: female • 15 days fledging • Time until independent unknown*

Finch family *(Fringillidae)*

BULLFINCH
Pyrrhula pyrrhula
Length: 14.5 cm (5³/₄ in)

Willow catkins – *spring food*

Black cap

White rump

THE BULLFINCH CAN easily pass unnoticed in the garden because it keeps to thick foliage. Even if you flush one out, often all you catch sight of is a flash of white rump. There are many gardeners who dislike bullfinches because of the damage they can do in spring to fruit-tree buds and blossom and, later, to soft fruit and peas. The bullfinch's preferred winter diet is seeds but when stocks run out it turns to eating buds, even though these contain little nourishment.

MALE

Recognition The male has deep pink under-parts. (The female is greyer.)

FEEDING Bullfinches mainly eat the seeds of ash, birch, dock, nettle and bramble, but they also rip buds off trees. During the breeding season insects are fed to the nestlings.
Bird-table Bullfinches occasionally feed on peanuts and assorted seeds.

FEMALE

Greyish underparts

VOICE The song is a quiet warbling. The call is a distinc-tive whistling *deu-deu*, which you can hear plainly, even when the birds are hidden.

NESTING Unlike most other garden birds, pairs stay together through the year rather than split up after breeding. In spring, the male takes the initiative in choosing the nest site. He leads the female to suitable locations in a thick hedge or conifer but she builds the delicate nest of fine twigs and rootlets.

Fledgling A bullfinch, just out of the nest, perches among rose hips. It has brownish plumage and lacks the distinctive black cap.

Nesting information *April – August • 2 broods • 4 or 5 purple-streaked, green-blue eggs • 14 days incubation: female • 12–16 days fledging • 2–3 weeks until independent*

Sparrow family *(Passeridae)*

HOUSE SPARROW

Passer domesticus
Length: 14.5 cm (5³/₄ in)

THE HOUSE SPARROW deserves its name. It rarely nests away from buildings, although it occasionally nests in holes in trees and rock faces, or usurps the nests of other birds, such as martins and swallows. Less often, it makes its own domed nest of grasses in a tree or hedge. Exploiting human settlements for shelter and food has enabled house sparrows to spread all over the world.

MALE

Black bib

Recognition
The male has brown upper-parts, streaked with black, and grey cheeks, crown and rump.

Other sparrows Watch out for tree sparrows: unlike the house sparrow, they lack the grey crown and rump, and have a brown spot in the middle of each cheek.

VOICE The house sparrow has a variety of persistent *cheep* and *chirp* calls, and a song that is a medley of these calls.

Song *A male (left) chirps monotonously to try to attract a mate.*

Garden disturbance A common sight in spring is a group of sparrows chasing each other across the garden, chirruping wildly, and ending up in a tree where they mill about, apparently fighting. It is difficult to see precisely what is happening but the object of excitement is a female and the other participants are males who are courting her. She will try to fend them off, aided by her mate.

Centre of attention *The female is more uniformly brown, lacking the grey on rump and crown and the black on the head and throat. (Juveniles resemble the female.)*

FEMALE

Nettle *The common stinging nettle, although trouble for the gardener, will provide a meal of seeds for the house sparrow.*

FEEDING The house sparrow is basically a seed-eater but it eats a wide mixture of animal and plant food, including shoots and flowers. House sparrows are pests on farms, stealing grain from standing crops, and wherever they have access to human food. Urban sparrows used to rely on grain spilt from horses' nosebags but they now do well on the increasing amount of edible litter. Animal food is needed for feeding to the nestlings. Look out for house sparrows chasing flies across the lawn, gorging on greenfly and even picking insects out of spiders' webs.

Nutrition *A female sparrow takes some scraps of food from a hanging basket.*

Seed-eaters *House sparrows feed on seeds and edible litter in a city park.*

NESTING The usual nesting site is a hole or crevice in a building. Thatched houses provide attractive sites, so wire netting is used to keep sparrows from burrowing into the thatch. After nesting has finished, pairs of house sparrows continue to use the nest as a snug roost throughout the winter. (The young birds roost together in evergreens and among ivy. You can see them gathering in late afternoon and hear them twittering conversationally in the foliage until darkness falls.)
Nest-box House sparrows readily use enclosed nest-boxes (p.115) and may even displace tits from them.

Bird-table House sparrows can be a problem in gardens because flocks clear bird-tables of all forms of scraps. Despite this, there is much of interest in their habits. They are quick to learn new ways of finding food, following the example of tits in stealing milk from bottles and learning to feed from tit-bells (p.119) and peanut bags.

Feathering the nest *A male perches on a wire with material for his nest, which may be built in a hole in a building.*

Nesting information *March – September* • *2– 4 broods* • *3–5 brown-blotched, white eggs* • *14 days incubation: mainly female* • *15 days fledging* • *1 week until independent*

Starling family *(Sturnidae)*

STARLING

Sturnus vulgaris
Length: 22 cm (8½ in)

THE STARLING IS SO widespread that fruit-growers consider it a pest, as do people in cities because it fouls buildings on which it roosts. A bold nature coupled with a voracious appetite has not made starlings popular in the garden, because they clear the bird-table before other birds can claim their share. Yet their lively behaviour makes starlings attractive birds to watch as they perform a repertoire of fascinating activities.

Recognition *In winter, starlings have spangled plumage. This starling in its first winter has lost the mouse-brown juvenile plumage.*

Buff-speckled above

Glossy plumage

White-speckled below

Scene at dusk
Just before dusk, you can see large numbers of starlings meeting in trees before they fly to their communal roost.

Flight *In summer, starlings hawk for flying insects. Pointed wings and a short, square tail give the starling an arrowhead silhouette in flight.*

Flocks For much of the year starlings live in flocks. They feed together, so there is often a rush of starlings to the bird-table. After breeding, thousands swarm to join vast communal roosts. In the evening, you can hear a chorus of noisy squeals as they fly overhead in close formation.

Plumage The starling's glossy, blackish feathers are shot with metallic blues, purples and greens. After the summer moult, the buff and white tips to new feathers create an attractive, spangled appearance, most marked in young birds.

Spring plumage *The plumage has lost much of its spotted appearance because the pale tips of the feathers have worn away.*

Long, pointed beak (brown in winter)

Singing out *A male sings, throat-feathers raised and wings flapping, from a prominent perch to attract a mate to his nest site.*

VOICE The song is a medley of rattles, squeaks and whistles, often with mimicked notes of other species, including curlew, pheasant and tawny owl. When singing at high intensity, the throat-feathers are raised and part-spread wings are waved. Singing occurs at communal roosts as well as in the territory. Calls include an aggressive *chacker-chacker* and a harsh, screaming distress call

Lawn food *A starling extracts a leatherjacket.*

Bird-table Put out bread, scraps, hanging bones and peanut bags for starlings.

NESTING The male builds a rough nest of grass, which is lined by the female, in a hole in a tree or building. He may also decorate it with green leaves and flower petals collected from plants with insecticidal properties. The drawback with open-beak feeding (described above) is that to collect a good beakful for the nestlings, a starling has to drop one item of food before probing for the next. Later, fledglings are brought to the lawn and food is crammed directly into their beaks.
Nest-box Large enclosed box (p.115).

FEEDING Starlings visit the garden for a wide variety of animal and plant foods. Their main food is earthworms, leatherjackets (the larvae of craneflies) and other small creatures found near grass roots. They stride forward in a group, inspecting the ground with frequent, rapid thrusts of their beaks. The beak is equipped with strong muscles for forcing it open at each probe into the soil. Swivelling its eyes forwards to peer down the hole, the starling will focus on the end of its beak to identify anything worth eating. At the same time, it is still able to scan around for any lurking predators, such as cats.

Meal-time *A parent brings small insects and spiders to its young beneath the roof of a house.*

Nesting information *April – May • 1 or 2 broods • 4 or 5 pale greenish-blue eggs • 12 days incubation: female • 21 days fledging • 4–5 weeks until independent*

Crow family *(Corvidae)*

JAY

Garrulus glandarius

Length: 34 cm (13½ in)

Pale blue wing-patch

Streaked crown
The crown can be raised into a crest, giving a domed appearance to the head.

White rump

Pinkish-fawn body

THE MOST COLOURFUL member of the crow family, the jay is becoming a regular visitor to rural and suburban gardens where there are plenty of mature trees. It is often shy and, in its natural woodland home, usually gives away its presence only by its harsh *krar* cries, but it may be seen as it flaps jerkily and heavily across clearings on its broad wings. Jays visit bird-tables most readily in the early morning before people are about.

VOICE Rasping *krar* sounds are used as alarm calls and in social inter-actions. There are a number of quieter guttural and warbling notes. Jays are good mimics and imitate other crows, tawny owls and even birdsong.

Flight *When flying away, black wings and tail contrast with the white rump and white and pale blue wing-patches.*

Retrieving acorns
Jays bury surplus acorns and can remember where they have been buried even through 30 cm (12 in) of snow.

FEEDING Acorns are the important food for most of the year. Jays also eat other seeds and fruit, as well as insects (in particular, beetles and caterpillars) and occasionally mice and voles.

Bird-table Jays come for vegetable scraps, which they carry away to eat or bury. Some have learnt to take peanuts from mesh bags or wire spiral dispensers.

NESTING Both sexes build the untidy nest in a tree or tall shrub, usually at some height above the ground. It is mainly composed of twigs broken off trees, bound together with earth, and lined with roots, hair and fibres. Jays sometimes rob small birds' nests, perhaps only when they have young to feed.

Nesting information *May – June • 1 brood • 3–7 brown-flecked, greenish eggs • 16–17 days incubation: female • 21–23 days fledging • 8 weeks until independent*

Crow family *(Corvidae)*

MAGPIE
Pica pica
Length: 46 cm (18 in)

Plumage *There is a greenish gloss to the black and white feathers.*

THE MOST UNPOPULAR garden bird, the magpie is damned for keeping watch on garden song-birds to locate their nests and then ravage them. Yet it is unfair to single out the magpie as even tits and thrushes occasionally kill other birds. A magpie "wedding" starts when a pair tries to carve out a new territory from an established one. The residents attempt to drive the interlopers out and the noise of the chase attracts other magpies.

VOICE A harsh *kyack* or a repeated *shak-shak-shak* of alarm is often the first sign of a magpie's presence.

20–25 cm (8–10 in) long tail

Scrap
A magpie feeds on meat.

FEEDING
Like most crows, the magpie eats almost anything: beetles, grasshoppers, slugs, snails, woodlice and spiders, and many seeds and fruit. The nestlings of other birds, animal road casualties and injured birds are easy meals.
Bird-table Meat and bread scraps.

NESTING The nest is a substantial structure of sticks and twigs, lined with mud and plant material, and is usually built in a tree or tall shrub. In areas of Europe, magpies nest on buildings or electricity pylons. The family stays near the nest for several days after fledging. The young remain in a loose flock.

Magpie nest
The domed nest has a single side-opening and is roofed over with thorns as a protection against predatory attacks by other crows.

Nesting information *March – May • 1 or 2 broods • 5–7 speckled, greenish eggs • 22 days incubation: female • 22–27 days fledging • Time until independent unknown*

Crow family (*Corvidae*)

CARRION CROW

Corvus corone

Length: 47 cm (18½ in)

Strong, black bill

LIKE OTHER MEMBERS of the crow family, the carrion crow is shy of people. If not persecuted, it becomes tame enough to search for food in gardens, which unfortunately includes the eggs and nestlings of small birds. While adult crows live in their territories, the non-breeding young gather in flocks. The carrion crow may interbreed with the hooded crow, a race of the carrion crow (distinguished by its grey body) which lives in northern and western Europe, including Scotland and Ireland.

Recognition *The carrion crow is all black, without the bare, grey face of the rook.*

VOICE There is a number of caws. A repeated *kraa-kraa-kraa* is the male's "song" and is given while jerking the head up and spreading the tail. You can hear an angry *ark-ark* during territorial disputes, and a longer *kaaar* when the crow is alarmed.

Acorn *– part of a varied diet*

FEEDING The crow eats a broad range of food, including carrion, grain, acorns, potatoes, insects and their larvae, snails, worms and the eggs and nestlings of other birds. Surplus food is hoarded.
Bird-table Bread, meat, potatoes and other kitchen scraps attract crows.

Hunting *A crow scans the lawn for worms.*

NESTING The substantial nest, built by both sexes high in a tree fork, is made of three layers: an outer cup of twigs; a middle layer of fine twigs, roots, earth and grass; and a lining of hair and bark fibres. While the female incubates the eggs, the male stands guard, warning her of danger as well as bringing food to her.

Nesting information *March – June • 1 brood • 4 or 5 brown-speckled, greenish eggs • 17–19 days incubation: female • 32–36 days fledging • 4 weeks until independent*

Crow family *(Corvidae)*

ROOK
Corvus frugilegus
Length: 46 cm (18 in)

SUPERFICIALLY SIMILAR TO the carrion crow, the rook is more sociable. It flies in large and ragged flocks and feeds communally in fields. Too wary to be a common garden bird, the rook will visit if you have a quiet country garden near a *rookery* (breeding colony), especially in the early morning and where a tall tree gives it a safe perch. It visits rubbish dumps in towns

Throat pouch
The bulging pouch (beneath the base of the bill) is used for carrying food.

VOICE The rook makes a raucous *kaah*. The song is a mixture of soft caws, rattles and cackles.

Untidy feathers around legs

Recognition
Unlike the crow, the adult rook has bare skin in front of the eyes. A raised crest highlights the steep forehead.

FEEDING Rooks eat earthworms and insects, such as leatherjackets, beetles and caterpillars, as well as grain, acorns and fruit. Nests of small birds are robbed. Like other crows, rooks hoard surplus food.
Bird-table Rooks enjoy feeding on hanging bones, fat and cooked meat.

NESTING The rookery is usually at the top of a clump of tall trees: nests are often built close together but one or two may be on their own. Each nest is built by both sexes of twigs, grasses and mud and lined with finer plant material. The male brings food in his throat pouch to the female when she is incubating.

Tree-top nests *The social life is based on the rookery, although young rooks flock and roost separately in autumn and winter.*

Nesting information   *Late February – June   •   1 brood   •   3–5 speckled, greenish eggs   •   16–18 days incubation: female   •   32–33 days fledging   •   4 weeks until independent*

Crow family *(Corvidae)*

JACKDAW
Corvus monedula
Length: 33 cm (13 in)

ASOCIABLE AND ENTERTAINING bird, the jackdaw can be seen in many towns and villages, where it nests in buildings and old trees. In northern Europe, jackdaws often roost in towns during the winter but commute each day to feed in the countryside. Bright button eyes give the jackdaw an air of sagacity – experiments have shown that members of the crow family are among the most intelligent birds.

Grey hood

Bluish sheen on black plumage

Recognition *Jackdaws are smaller than the other black-coloured members of the crow family.*

VOICE The sharp *tchak* is a familiar contact call, but there is also a *chaair* note that is given in flight. The song comprises a medley of *tchaks* and other notes.

Aerobatic flier *Jackdaws are agile in the air, sometimes performing aerobatics, apparently just for fun.*

Social life The jackdaw is a sociable bird. Flocks of jackdaws fly and feed with other species, such as rooks (when they can be distinguished by their smaller size and *tchak* cries) and starlings. Mated pairs of jackdaws fly together.

Glossy, black wings

Young jackdaw *The juvenile bird* (left) *is a duller colour than the adult and shows less contrast between the hood and the body.*

Thieves Jackdaws are notorious for stealing bright objects, especially glittering jewellery. The habit is immortalized in Richard Harris Barham's *The Jackdaw of Rheims*, a nineteenth-century poem that tells of the jackdaw that stole the cardinal's ring.

All that glitters The thief of the bird world steals an earring. Jackdaws occasionally steal inedible objects, particularly if they are shiny, for no purpose.

FEEDING Jackdaws eat all sorts of vege-table and animal foods, mainly cereals, fruit and insects but they also steal eggs and nestlings from the nests of other birds. They usually feed on the ground and, being less wary, reach food before the larger rooks and crows arrive at the scene and drive them away.

Bird-table The jackdaw comes into your garden or yard to take a variety of scraps from the bird-table or the ground. In the garden, it shows the same enthusiasm that it has when scavenging in streets and raiding litterbins in parks. Try putting out fat and bones, especially in the early morning when few people are about.

Ground feeder Jackdaws search on the ground among stones and logs for a variety of large insects, such as these ground beetles, which are a high-protein food.

NESTING Jackdaws nest in colonies, usually choosing holes in buildings or tree trunks as nest sites. They sometimes take over old nests of larger birds or build in gaps in dense foliage or even in the chimney pots of occupied houses. The nest may be employed for roosting throughout the year. Both the parents build the nest from sticks, often accumulating huge quantities of them, and line it inside with hair, bark, rags and other materials, mixed together with earth.

Nest-box A jackdaw will nest in a secluded, large enclosed nest-box (p.115).

Hunger A jackdaw nestling begs for food.

Nesting information April – June • 1 brood • 4 or 5 spotted, pale blue eggs • 17–18 days incubation: female • 30–35 days fledging • Time until independent unknown

CHAPTER THREE

ATTRACTING BIRDS

A GARDEN WILL BE visited by birds only
if it offers some of the necessities of life.
Every bird needs three fundamental things for
its well-being – food, water and shelter. If some
of these basics can be found in the garden,
they make a visit worthwhile and increase
the birds' chances of survival. You cannot
guarantee that these provisions will be naturally
available in your garden, but there are many
ways that you can artificially reproduce them.
Putting out food on bird-tables, filling a bird-
bath with water and providing nest-boxes for
roosting and nesting all create a bird-friendly
environment. This chapter describes birdfeeders
(together with the food to put on them) as well
as bird-baths and nest-boxes that you can
either make or buy. Hints on their construction
and use will help you improve your
garden with birds in mind.

A blue tit appreciating a bird-bath

·: WHAT BIRDS NEED :·

Your success in attracting birds depends on how closely you can fulfil their basic needs. Even if your garden does not contain a natural wealth of food, a water supply or large, mature trees for nest sites, you can still copy these features in the garden by providing food, birdfeeders, bird-baths and nest-boxes. Knocking together pieces of wood for nest-boxes and birdfeeders provides the chance to satisfy a creative, do-it-yourself urge. Moreover, they are a great place to start for the novice woodworker. The birds will not mind if the construction is less than perfect, and only a little practice and application is needed to solve the Christmas present problem. Your efforts will not take you long and will be quickly appreciated.

· FEEDING THE BIRDS ·

Feeding the birds is a pastime that ranges from casually throwing crusts out of the kitchen window to distributing commercial quantities of food in a battery of feeding devices. Food you provide for birds not only keeps them well fed but also reduces the amount of energy they have to spend searching for a meal. This can be important in the winter cold or when there are young to feed in summer.

The amount of money and effort you put into feeding birds depends on your level of interest and the time you can devote to watching them. My birdfeeder array is strategically positioned outside my study window and, to provide a welcome distraction from work, I ensure that there is always enough food throughout the day to keep the birds coming. Furthermore, I am making some systematic studies of who uses the bird-table, so I have every excuse to gaze out of the window.

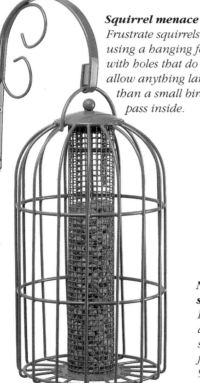

Squirrel menace
Frustrate squirrels by using a hanging feeder with holes that do not allow anything larger than a small bird to pass inside.

New stainless steel feeder
Designed to attract a wide range of small birds. The feeder holds over 900 g (2 lb) of peanuts.

· WINTER FOOD ·

It is often said that once you start putting out food for birds in winter, you should not stop until spring arrives, and that if you cannot guarantee a continuous supply, it is best not to start at all. This strikes me as rather strict and unnecessary. While birdfeeders make life much easier for birds and contribute to their survival in hard weather, no bird relies entirely on one food source. In natural circumstances, birds have to adapt to changing food stocks and their livelihood depends on quickly finding new supplies.

Yet there are two situations in which birds may become dependent on birdfeeders. In unusually harsh spells, when natural food is unobtainable, well-stocked birdfeeders are definite life-savers. As these periods do not last long, there is no need to provide supplies for months. And on large, new housing estates, especially where gardens are still rather bare, feeders help maintain a high population. Birds do not feed only in one garden: they have regular rounds through a neighbourhood, so if you are away on a holiday, the birds will simply bypass the empty bird-table until your return.

However, where feeders have been maintaining an unnaturally high population, a shortage of food could develop if the birds were forced back on to natural supplies, especially at the end of winter when stocks are low. I suspect that we simply do not know enough about the winter feeding habits of garden birds to make a strict ruling, but do not feel guilty if your feeders remain empty for a while.

Hopper *Even in winter, nuts* (left) *go uncollected if there is enough natural food available.*

Food source *A tit-bell* (right) *is a life-saver in hard times.*

· SUMMER FOOD ·

Many people stop feeding their birds in summer when some interesting birds, such as siskins and fieldfares, migrate to their breeding-grounds and others return to the countryside to nest. Those that remain tend to switch to natural foods and ignore the bird-table but, as discussed on page 16, the garden cannot be relied upon to be a good source of food. If you have coaxed tits and others to nest in

Summer scraps *Persuade a robin to stay in your garden over summer by continuing to place out food for it in a feeding bowl.*

Log-feeder *Food in summer* (above) *is appreciated by birds that stay in the garden.*

Scrap basket *Resume putting out supplies of food, such as bread and cheese* (right), *after the young birds have left the nest.*

your garden by putting up nest-boxes, it is reasonable to make sure that their families will have enough to eat.

The danger is that the nestlings may be fed unsuitable food, although some birds give their nestlings a different diet from their own anyway so they can still feed at the bird-table while finding natural food for their offspring. The problems come when natural food is scarce and the nestlings are stuffed with dry bread, coconut or peanuts, which can easily choke them. If you stop putting out food during nesting, do start again when the fledglings appear. They will benefit from easy meals and you may have the pleasure of seeing entire families of tits, nuthatches and even woodpeckers together at a birdfeeder.

· WATER ·

Pause to reflect *A marsh tit perches on the rim of a bird-bath before taking a drink.*

Birds need water for both drinking and bathing. Those species that feed on worms, caterpillars and other juicy animals do not need to drink as much as birds that live exclusively on a diet of dry seeds, but a supply of water is always welcome. Putting a bird-bath in your garden is another incentive for birds to visit because water is required all year round.

The bird-bath is very popular during hot summer weather when birds need to keep cool and when puddles and pools have dried up in the drought. Birds do not sweat as we do but pant to keep cool, rather like dogs, by evaporating water from their mouths and lungs. However, contrary to popular assumption, birds use the bird-bath more frequently in winter than in summer because it becomes a vital reservoir of drinking water when frequent frosts seal off natural supplies.

You can sometimes see birds taking mouthfuls of snow to get water but this is rather like eating ice cream in a blizzard. It takes 12 times as much heat to melt a gram of ice as it does to warm the same amount of water to body heat. So just keeping the bird-bath clear of ice will help the birds at a time when saving energy is so important. Birds also like to bathe in frosty weather because they must maintain their plumage in peak condition to keep warm. If birds cannot find water, both their flight efficiency and insulation will be impaired. This will cost them dearly in wasted energy.

· NEST SITES ·

Even in a mature garden that is well stocked with trees, dense climbers or shrubs, there is likely to be a shortage of suitable nest sites. This is especially true if large numbers of local birds have been maintained through the winter by free handouts at birdfeeders.

A few birds will nest in hidden corners and raise families. Nest-boxes bring more birds into the garden and make it easier for you to follow the unfolding saga of birds' family lives, while the birds' invest-ment of time and energy is less likely to end in disaster. Although some birds, especially the finches, never use nest-boxes, hole-nesters, such as tits and starlings, eagerly accept them.

The nest-box must be sited at least 1.8 m (6 ft) above the ground, away from the worst effects of the sun and rain, for

Metal plate (right) *If there is a danger of squirrels and woodpeckers enlarging a tit-box entrance, nail a metal plate around the hole.*

example, under a tree canopy. It should be secure enough not to fall down, but it does not matter if it wobbles a little.

Resist the temptation to visit the nest-box too often – the laying period is a particularly sensitive time. If nestlings are disturbed when they are well-grown, they are likely to "explode" out of the nest. If they do, gently prod them back into the box and stuff the hole with a handker-chief until they settle down.

Timing *Put up your nest-box before New Year: this allows it to weather and gives early-pairing birds a chance to inspect it and roost there.*

·: BIRD-TABLES AND FEEDERS :·

THERE IS A WIDE variety of birdfeeding devices on the market, suitable for all kinds of taste and garden situation. Making your own is much more satisfying, and few tools and little skill are needed to turn out acceptable products. Birdfeeders bring birds to eye-level, giving you the opportunity to observe all the birds' excitement as they jostle for food. Site the feeder out of full sun and in a sheltered location, preferably near suitable perches. Take care to place the feeder away from cover where cats can wait in ambush. Add a low roof to prevent rain sweeping away the food. When building the birdfeeders, follow either the metric or imperial measurements given below: it is not possible to swap between the two.

· OPEN BIRD-TABLE ·

The open bird-table is the traditional way to provide food for birds. It is easy to make, consisting of a board held up on a post or hung from a branch or bracket with chains. Use the dimensions for the floor of the covered bird-table (shown opposite). Cut the base of the tray from a sheet of 12 mm (¹/₂ in) plywood and make the rim from lengths of 20 mm (³/₄ in) square wood. Fix these side pieces with 30 mm (1¹/₄ in) nails. Reduce the chance of squirrels reaching the table by attaching an inverted biscuit tin or conical piece of metal near the top of the post.

Low rim *The surrounding edges help to prevent food being scattered, but leave gaps at the corners to let rainwater drain away.*

Feeding tray *For ground-feeders, such as wrens, support the tray on short legs.*

Screw

Wooden blocks *Nail small blocks to the centre of the underside of the tray to make a seating for the supporting post.*

Post *Support the tray on top of a post, about 1.5 m (5 ft) in length. Make the post from smooth wood (or use a galvanized iron pole) and attach the anti-predator devices. Firmly drive the post in and then screw on the table through the blocks.*

Hook

Log-feeder *To entertain woodpeckers, nuthatches and tits (p.94) hang a log-feeder from your bird-table.*

Holes *Drill holes through the log and stuff them with fat.*

· COVERED BIRD-TABLE ·

Once you have made an open bird-table it is quite simple to add a roof, which keeps the food dry and provides a place for a hanging seed hopper. Make the roof from 9 mm (³/₈ in) ply and angle one long edge of each roof piece. Cut the uprights from 20 mm (³/₄ in) square wood: angle both ends of each upright by sawing off wedges, 4 mm (¹/₈ in) from the bottom and 6 mm (¹/₄ in) from the top.

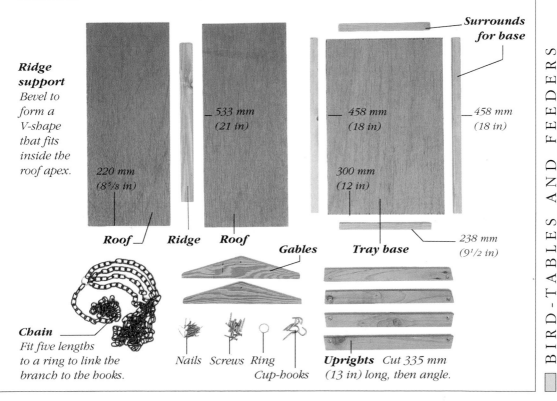

Cup-hooks

Gables
Cut triangular shapes, 300 mm (12 in) wide and 60 mm (2¹/₂ in) tall. Fix to the uprights, then screw in the ridge.

Assembly Nail the uprights to the inside corners of the tray. The uprights will not be vertical – they should slant slightly outwards. Attach the gables and fit in the ridge. Fasten on the roof pieces, making sure the angled edges fit together at the apex.

Hanging table
Screw four cup-hooks through the corners of the roof and into the gable ends. Hang from a branch on chains. The table can also be fixed on a post.

Front view

Ridge support
Bevel to form a V-shape that fits inside the roof apex.

220 mm
(8⁵/₈ in)

Roof

533 mm
(21 in)

Ridge

Roof

Gables

Surrounds for base

458 mm
(18 in)

458 mm
(18 in)

300 mm
(12 in)

Tray base

238 mm
(9¹/₂ in)

Chain
Fit five lengths to a ring to link the branch to the hooks.

Nails Screws Ring
Cup-hooks

Uprights Cut 335 mm (13 in) long, then angle.

·BIRD PUDDING HOLDER·

If you decide to make your bird pudding (p.106) in an old food tin, you can either directly turn the pudding out on to the bird-table or else simply build a special holder for the tin. The holder, which can be nailed to a post or tree trunk, not only keeps the bird pudding dry but also guarantees that it lasts longer because it is not so easy for birds to break off and carry away large chunks. The small screws that fasten the tin in place can easily be removed to release the tin, so it can be refilled with bird pudding. To ensure the top edge of the tin is not jagged or sharp, and does not cut the birds, use a tin opener that leaves a smooth, blunt edge. This feeder holds a 450 g (1 lb) tin; if you use a tin of a different size adjust the dimensions given below accordingly. Cut out the pieces of wood from 20 mm (³/₄ in) thick floorboard or plywood.

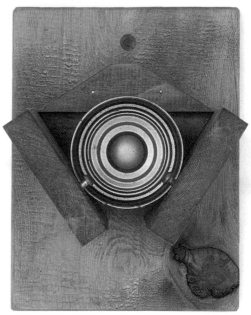

Steadying brace
The base of the brace is 125 mm (5 in) long, and is notched to fit over the can.

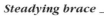

Hole *Allows holder to be nailed to a tree*

Front view *The tin can is secured in position between the two side supports by the 15 mm (⁵/₈ in) screws.*

Side view

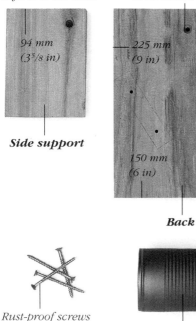

94 mm (3³/₈ in)

Side support

225 mm (9 in)

150 mm (6 in)

Back

125 mm (5 in)

Side support

Drilled holes

Assembly Mark the position of the side supports on the back piece, and drill holes for the four long screws. Fix on the sides by screwing through the back and nail on the steadying brace. Fit the tin between supports. Make a pilot hole in each of the side pieces to take the small screws. Turn the screws until they hold the tin in place.

Rust-proof screws 60 mm (2¹/₂ in)

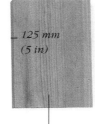

Empty tin can

Screws 15 mm (⁵/₈ in)

Oval nails 30 mm (1¹/₄ in)

·SCRAP BASKET·

A scrap basket filled with kitchen left-overs (pp.102–3) or various nuts (p.107) is appreciated by many different birds. The simplest container is a netting bag that stops scraps being blown about, but the food soon becomes sodden and the bag messy. It is quite easy to make a refillable basket that will keep the food dry. Use galvanized wire or plastic-coated mesh to cover the front and base of the basket; 20 mm (³/₄ in) floorboard for the sides, back, brace and batten; and 12 mm (¹/₂ in) ply for the lid. Attach the lid with a 105 mm (4¹/₈ in) length of piano hinge.

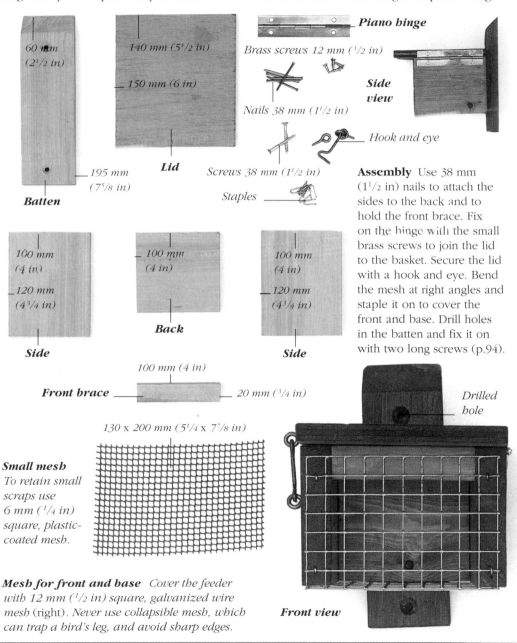

60 mm (2¹/₂ in)

Batten

140 mm (5¹/₂ in)

150 mm (6 in)

195 mm (7⁵/₈ in)

Lid

Piano hinge

Brass screws 12 mm (¹/₂ in)

Nails 38 mm (1¹/₂ in)

Side view

Screws 38 mm (1¹/₂ in)

Staples

Hook and eye

100 mm (4 in)

120 mm (4³/₄ in)

Side

100 mm (4 in)

Back

100 mm (4 in)

100 mm (4 in)

120 mm (4³/₄ in)

Side

100 mm (4 in)

Front brace ___ *20 mm (³/₄ in)*

130 x 200 mm (5¹/₄ x 7⁷/₈ in)

Small mesh
To retain small scraps use 6 mm (¹/₄ in) square, plastic-coated mesh.

Assembly Use 38 mm (1¹/₂ in) nails to attach the sides to the back and to hold the front brace. Fix on the hinge with the small brass screws to join the lid to the basket. Secure the lid with a hook and eye. Bend the mesh at right angles and staple it on to cover the front and base. Drill holes in the batten and fix it on with two long screws (p.94).

Drilled hole

Mesh for front and base *Cover the feeder with 12 mm (¹/₂ in) square, galvanized wire mesh (right). Never use collapsible mesh, which can trap a bird's leg, and avoid sharp edges.*

Front view

• SEED HOPPER •

A hopper is the most practical way to provide seeds as it keeps them dry and stops the wind blowing them away. Other methods tend to be wasteful, although ground-feeding birds, such as chaffinches and dunnocks, prefer their seeds broad-cast on the lawn. This hopper, which uses a 450 g (1 lb) jam jar, is simple to make. Using the dimensions given (altering as necessary for a different jar size), cut the base from 25 mm (1 in) wood, the side surrounds from 20 mm (³/4 in) square wood and the back from 12 mm (¹/2 in) plywood. When the hopper is built, fill the jar with seeds, or nuts, and invert it. (Cover the jar with a piece of card to pre-vent spillage while you are fitting it into place.) You can adjust the height of the jar above the tray to regulate the flow of different sizes of seed.

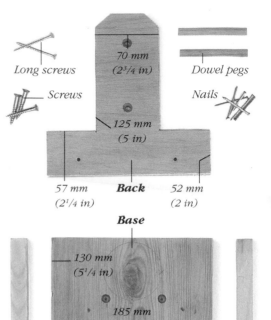

Long screws

70 mm
(2³/4 in)

Dowel pegs

Screws

Nails

125 mm
(5 in)

57 mm
(2¹/4 in)

Back

52 mm
(2 in)

Base

130 mm
(5¹/4 in)

185 mm
(7¹/4 in)

Side surround (with mitred corners)

Webbing and tacks

Jam jar

Back piece
When the hopper is completed, tack both ends of the webbing to the back piece. Fix the hopper to a tree trunk through two holes drilled in the back (p.93).

Gaps *Leave gaps in the surround for water drainage.*

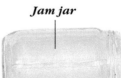

Front view

Dowel pegs
Two wooden pegs steady the jar.

Elastic webbing
Secure the jar with webbing that allows it to be removed for refilling.

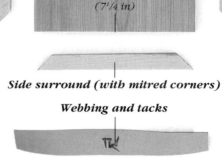

Assembly Fix the back on to the base using the long screws. Then, nail on the side surrounds, leaving gaps at the corners. Drill two holes in the base to take the 80 mm (3¹/8 in) long dowels. Screw three small screws under the rim of the jar to raise it off the base and let seeds fall out. To alter the size of the gap, turn the screws either clockwise or anti-clockwise.

· WINDOW FEEDER ·

You do not need a garden to attract birds. Use this feeder, which attaches to a window-sill, to see the entertaining activity of the bird-table at close quarters. Even in built-up areas you can at least rely on blackbirds, starlings and sparrows to pay a visit. The window feeder combines three different types of feeder. The feeding tray (p.96) has a narrow, oblong-shaped base to fit along the width of the window. The design of the scrap basket (p.99) has been slightly modified: a wedge-shaped basket, of the same width as the feeding tray, leaves more space on the tray. Cover the front of the basket with mesh and hinge the lid. The seed hopper (p.100) has been altered because its separate base is unnecessary. The jar is held by a detachable webbing strap, to enable the jar to be refilled easily. Two blocks nailed on to the back piece replace the dowels.

Wedge-shaped scrap basket

Seed hopper *The jar is fixed with detachable webbing, secured by a small peg.*

Attachment to the window-sill
Hook the feeder to the sill so that one side of the table is against the front edge of the sill and the back of the bracket rests against the wall.

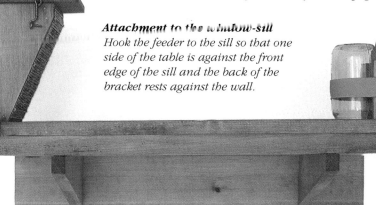

Side view

Hanging the feeder *Build a bracket to support the feeder. To make a rigid fixing, extend the bracket under the sill so that it is braced against the wall. Screw hooks into the front edge of the sill and eyes to match in the side of the tray that faces the window.*

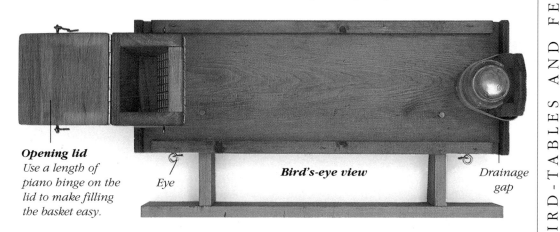

Opening lid
Use a length of piano hinge on the lid to make filling the basket easy.

Eye

Bird's-eye view

Drainage gap

Kitchen window-sill *Place this feeder outside the kitchen window and then you can simply throw out leftovers and kitchen scraps to tempt many different kinds of bird.*

·∴ BIRD-TABLE FARE ∵·

· KITCHEN SCRAPS ·

BIRDS NEED FOODS RICH in carbohydrates and fats to help them build up the vital reserves of body fat that they need to survive long, cold nights. Many kitchen scraps have a high fat content and are ideal bird food – suet, bone marrow, dripping, stale cheese, bacon rind, cake and pastry. However, to avoid the possible spread of diseases, only put out bones and meat that have been cooked. (Always ensure that poultry bones are out of the reach of cats or dogs.) Never give birds desiccated coconut or uncooked rice as these can swell up inside the bird, often with fatal results. For this reason it is also best to soak dry bread in water before leaving it out on the bird-table.

Stale cake

Crusts and crumbs
Bread is the food most often put out for birds. It is not the best choice as it is not very nutritious but, as with humans, it helps fill empty stomachs. Stale cake and broken pieces from the bottom of the biscuit tin are more suitable as they are rich in fat. Put out fine crumbs for shy species, such as dunnocks and wrens.

Breadcrumbs and crusts

Broken biscuit

Cooked potatoes Potatoes in their jackets, which have been split open, last well as the soft contents can only be carried away a beakful at a time, and the skins take a long time to pick clean.

Uncooked pastry

Cooked spaghetti

Rice, pasta and pastry
Leftovers of cooked rice and spaghetti, and any uncooked pastry remains from your baking, are all rich in starch and will keep starlings and rooks busy.

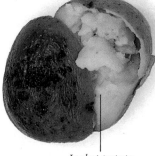

Jacket potato

Cooked rice

Fruit In late summer, fruit attracts birds as well as butterflies, bees and wasps. Gather some of the windfalls in autumn and store them in a cool, dark place. In the dead of winter, when birds have exhausted the natural supplies of fruit and berries, put the windfalls on the lawn, together with fruit you have bought that is past its prime. Or else, cut the fruit into pieces or impale it on spikes on the bird-table. Blackbirds, fieldfares, redwings, starlings and smaller birds such as black-caps, robins and blue tits all enjoy fruit.

Apple

Pear

Dry cheese Cheese that has dried out and become hard is ideal for birds, although the blue varieties and strongly flavoured ones tend to be left. For smaller species, such as the goldcrest, crumble or grate the cheese into little pieces. In cold weather, wrens, which do not visit the bird-table, appreciate cheese crumbs sprinkled among leaf litter. Stale cheese also makes an excellent ingredient of bird pudding (p.106).

Stale cheese

Fat and meat Put lumps of fat, bacon rind or fat trimmed off chops on to the bird-table. Melt large lumps of fat or dripping to pour over branches or into a log-feeder (p.96) or tit-bell. Hang cooked lumps of meat or meat bones, with shreds of meat and fat attached, to attract tits, starlings and woodpeckers as well as members of the crow family. Catfood is a gourmet food for birds!

Bacon rinds

Tinned catfood

Lard/cooking fat

Marrow bone

Meat bone

·GRAIN AND SEEDS·

GRAIN AND SEEDS PROVIDE birds with a valuable source of fats, carbohydrates, oils, minerals and vitamins. Some birds, such as the greenfinch and chaffinch, will eat almost any seeds from large cereal grains to small weed seeds, although sunflower seeds are the most popular of all. Other birds are more fastidious: siskins, for example, are particularly fond of niger seeds, whereas finches, tits and even pipits are attracted to hemp seeds. Pet shops sell ready-made seed mixes, which have been specially formulated to satisfy the appetites and nutritional needs of a wide variety of birds, but you can easily make up your own mixes at a much reduced cost. You can buy the grain and seeds individually and even supplement the mix with wild seeds (dock, thistle, stinging nettle, knapweed, teazel and ragwort) collected from the garden and dried. To avoid too much spillage serve the mixes from a seed hopper (p.100).

Popping corn This cereal grain is a useful source of oil and starch.

Pot barley The barley grain has a high bran, germ and vitamin content.

Wheat grain The whole grain is best as it contains valuable vitamins, minerals and fat, as well as fibre.

Rolled oats Oats are rich in protein and fats, but serve rolled oats as birds cannot easily remove the tough husks.

Hemp seeds These seeds are a favourite among tits and nuthatches, which hammer the seeds to crack them open.

Niger seeds Rich in oil, niger seeds come from the ramtil plant, which is cultivated in India.

Millet seeds These grass seeds have a high starch content and are a good source of minerals and vitamins.

Sunflower seeds A great bird food, sunflower seeds are very nutritious, being full of oil, protein and minerals.

Wild bird seeds This commercially available mixture contains a large range of seeds and grains that attracts larger birds.

Canary seed mix A proprietary mix, rich in canary seed, linseed, hemp and black rape, is suitable for small species of bird.

• MAKING FOOD •

IT IS EASY TO PREPARE food that brings birds to the bird-table. Bird pudding is quick to make and is an ideal way to use up kitchen scraps (although uncooked vegetables should not be included). Melt shredded suet, cooking fat or dripping in a pan to bind the pudding. It is generally unwise to give birds any food that is highly seasoned or strongly salted. Peanuts are very nutritious and they can be hung up on string, galvanized wire or in a mesh bag to attract a large number of birds. Make sure to buy high-quality peanuts that have been approved as bird food. Rearing your own mealworms requires a little more work but it is well worthwhile as robins may become hand-tame to take these delicacies. Mealworms are mobile and so should be served in a deep dish.

Seed pudding

Shredded suet

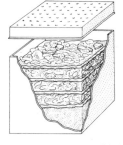

Fat ball

Suet stick

Nut pudding

Bird pudding You can either buy fat balls and suet sticks or make your own bird puddings. Half fill a tit-bell, coconut shell or tin (p.98) with a mixture of seeds, nuts, sultanas, cheese crumbs and cake scraps and then stir in almost the same amount of melted suet or fat to bind it. Allow the mixture to set solid before putting it out.

Mealworms The grubs, sold in pet shops, can be reared in a container filled with layers of bran and biscuit or dried bread. Keep the contents warm and just moist. The grubs pupate into beetles, which then lay eggs that hatch after about a week into more grubs. In a few weeks you will have a self-sustaining colony from which you can pick or sieve a crop of mealworms.

Tin box *A pierced lid lets the grubs breathe.*

Mealworms *These are larvae of a common brown beetle.*

Fresh, half-coconut

Peanuts in their shells, strung on a galvanized wire

Red mesh bag

Fruit and nuts A fresh, half-coconut, hung upside-down, is a great favourite of tits. Birds love all kinds of nut – for most species the nuts should be opened to allow the birds to get at the kernels but wood peckers and nuthatches can hammer shells apart. Nuts disappear quickly from feeders as birds take them away to hoard. Chop nuts to attract smaller species. Dried fruit can be added to bird pudding or, after soaking, placed on the bird-table.

Peanuts

Peanuts Because of their high fat and protein content, peanuts are a useful bird food. Thread peanuts in their shells on thin wire or string for tits, or put shelled, unsalted nuts in a mesh bag or wire container to attract greenfinches and other birds. In summer, grate whole nuts to prevent nestlings choking.

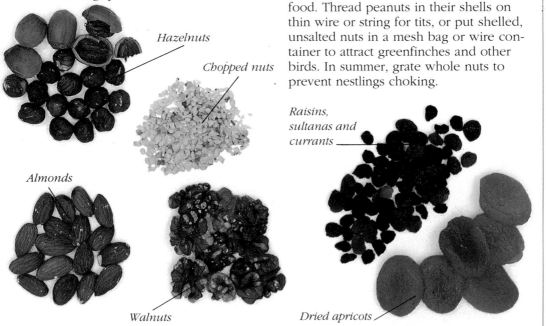

Hazelnuts

Chopped nuts

Almonds

Walnuts

Raisins, sultanas and currants

Dried apricots

∴ BIRD-BATHS AND PONDS ∴

THE BIRD-BATH IS a useful accessory to the birdfeeder array, because the resource of water is as necessary for birds as food. Birds come to the bird-bath throughout the year both to drink and bathe, while members of the crow family dunk hard food in the water to soften it. Bathing helps maintain the plumage and, in summer, keeps birds cool. Watching the activity at the bird-bath is entertaining and you will be able to identify several different species. Starlings and sparrows are the most frequent users and, as at the bird-table, these sociable birds crowd together around the water. Other regular visitors include blackbirds, blue tits, greenfinches, chaffinches, wrens and collared doves, but the bird-bath may also attract rarer birds, such as redpolls, hawfinches and crossbills.

• BIRD-BATHS •

Sundial *An expensive bath with a sundial has a classical feel, but it is no more likely to attract birds.*

There are many kinds of purpose-built bird-baths available from garden centres and pet shops, catering for different tastes. Some designs are more ornamental than practical. From a bird's point of view there are two major considerations: the bird-bath should have gently sloping sides, to allow small birds to paddle in and out easily, and a rough surface, so they can get a safe footing. Ideally, the bath should have a "deep end", 8–9 cm (3–3½ in) deep, which is large enough for a pigeon to soak itself or a flock of starlings to have a good splash without emptying all the water out of the bath.

You may be able to find a cheaper substitute in a hardware shop or you can easily make your own. An upside-down,

Cheap baths *Terracotta flower pot bases are ideal.*

Bath-time *A wren splashes about in a bath.*

galvanized dustbin lid, propped up on bricks, is often quoted as making an acceptable bird-bath, but the metal surface may be too slippery. Large dishes and flower pot bases are also possibilities. If the shape of container does not allow for both shallow and deep water, make an island from a stone. Alternatively, you can mould a simple and presentable bird-bath from mortar. Improvise the pedestal from a 7.5 cm (3 in) drainpipe or a pre-formed concrete post. Site the bird-bath near a tree where the birds can retire to dry and preen in safety. An ornamental bird-bath may well look attractive as a feature in the centre of the garden but this is usually not the best position for it.

MAKING A SIMPLE BIRD-BATH

Cut out a strip of hardboard. Nail the ends to a wooden block to form a girdle. Pour the mortar mix into the girdle. As it sets, shape it with a board or metal plate to form a shallow dish. Fix the bird-bath to a pedestal or lay it on the lawn.

· WATER IN WINTER ·

It is important to maintain a supply of water for birds during winter (p.95). Bathing is always followed by preening. Preening maintains the insulating properties of the plumage, which are vital for the survival of birds in cold weather, by keeping the feathers oiled and in tip-top condition. To guarantee birds access to water keep the bath clear of ice. A bath just off the ground, such as the upturned dustbin lid, may be kept ice-free by placing a slow-burning nightlight candle underneath it. You can rush out with kettles of boiling water to melt ice as it forms but it is easier to install an aquarium heater and thermostat, under a pile of gravel. If you expect prolonged, severe frosts, fit two heaters. All outdoor wiring must, of course, be waterproof. If you are in any doubt consult an electrician. Never use anti-freeze or salt to stop water freezing, as these will harm the birds.

· PONDS ·

An attractive alternative to a bird-bath is a pond. There are plenty of books that give technical information on the construction and stocking of garden ponds. These details are not relevant here – suffice it to say that the simplest way to install a pond is to buy a specially moulded fibre-glass container and the cheapest is to line a hole with thick polythene sheeting. In either case, the main problem is likely to be the disposal of the excavated soil! Whatever method you choose, the pond must be suitable for a bird to use. The edges should shelve away gently so that the bird can wade in up to its middle.

Kidney-shaped pond *Small birds can stand on the pile of stones to reach the water.*

A platform built from either bricks or stones, or a boggy shore, planted with marsh plants (like flag irises, bogbeans and marsh marigolds), provides an area of shallower water for small birds. Blackbirds and thrushes also appreciate the water-logged soil when building their nests.

∙: NEST-BOXES :∙

MAKING YOUR OWN NEST-BOX is great fun. You do not need any carpentry skills – birds cannot afford to be fussy about their housing standards. Select a nest-box that suits the birds living nearby. Do not make it too small: the box should have a minimum floor size of 100 cm² (16 in²) or the nestlings may become cramped and overheat on hot days. The best wood to use is either 15 cm (6 in) floorboard, 15 mm (⅝ in) thick, or a sheet of 15 mm (⅝ in) plywood, which should be treated with a harmless preservative. (Modify the dimensions according to the thickness of the timber you use.) To stop rain entering the box, seal the joints with glue or mastic, but as this may not make the box fully waterproof, drill drainage holes in the floor. Follow either metric or imperial measurements: do not mix the two.

∙ STANDARD BOXES ∙

Front view

Enclosed nest-box Small holes, such as the cavities found in old trees, are often in short supply in the garden. An enclosed box is a good substitute and blue and great tits usually visit a box within days of it being put up. Tack on a strip of waterproof material (inner tube or webbing is ideal) to hinge the lid, or if you do not intend to inspect the nest, simply screw the top down. To make a home exclusively for tits (a tit-box), make the entrance no more than 29 mm (1⅛ in) in diameter; otherwise, house sparrows and starlings may take over. Fix a metal plate around the hole to stop woodpeckers or squirrels enlarging it. Do not disturb the box until the fledglings have left; then open it and clean it out thoroughly. A soggy nest left inside harbours parasites and makes the box rot.

Side view
Secure the lid of the nest-box with a rust-proof hook and eye on each side. This allows you to clean out the box in autumn. It is best not to fit a perch as it encourages predators.

Entrance hole *Make the hole using an adjustable bit, or mark out the circle and then drill a series of holes around the inside of it, joining them up afterwards with a fret-saw.*

Front view

Open-fronted nest-box This box is a variation of the enclosed nest-box. It is used chiefly by robins and wrens, and, if much larger, occasionally kestrels. Instead of drilling an entrance hole, cut a panel to cover half the front of the box.

Preparation Both standard boxes are made in the same way. You need 1.8 m (6 ft) of 150 mm (6 in) floorboard, 15 mm ($^5/_8$ in) thick, or the equivalent amount of plywood. Make full-sized paper templates of the pieces using the measurements shown below. Arrange the templates on the wood before cutting out the pieces. The side edge of the lid that butts on to the back of the box (and the top edge of the front of the enclosed box) should be sawn at an angle so the lid fits tightly.

Log box *A natural-looking box can be made from a log. Halve the log and hollow it out, drill-ing a hole in one of the halves. To create the nesting chamber, simply nail the halves together. Add a piece for the roof.*

265 mm (10$^1/_2$ in)

Metal plate

Attachment hole

Nails
38 mm (1$^1/_2$ in)

150 mm (6 in)

312 mm (12$^1/_4$ in)

265 mm (10$^1/_2$ in)

Open front

Hooks and eyes

500 mm (20 in)

Hinge   **Tacks**

Side   **Front with hole**   **Side**

206 mm (8 in)

120 mm (4$^3/_4$ in)

Assembly Drill a small hole at the top and bottom of the back. With 38 mm (1$^1/_2$ in) nails, fix the sides of the box to the base, then attach the back and front. Finally nail the lid, or use 12 mm ($^1/_2$ in) tacks if it is hinged.

Base

Back

Lid

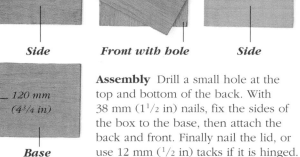

· TREECREEPER BOX ·

Front view

Treecreepers are not hole-nesters but they sometimes use specialized nest-boxes with side entrances. They will nest under a strip of curved bark, wired lengthways to a tree trunk, but you can build a more elaborate box. You will need a 1.4 m (5 ft) length of floorboard, 15 mm (5/8 in) thick, or a comparable amount of ply-wood. First make a paper template for all the pieces using the measurements shown below. Lay out the templates on the wood, ensuring that the two wedge-shaped pieces are arranged to make an oblong shape. Cut the pieces out and then, to ensure the lid is flush, saw the top edge of the front piece and the back edge of the lid at an angle. To make the entrances to the box cut away the top back corners of the sides as shown below.

Assembly Make attachment holes in the back piece. Nail the sides on to the back with 38 mm (1½ in) ovals. Next, slide in the front and secure it in place. Finally, using 145 mm (5½ in) of piano hinge and brass screws, attach the lid and fix on the hook and eye.

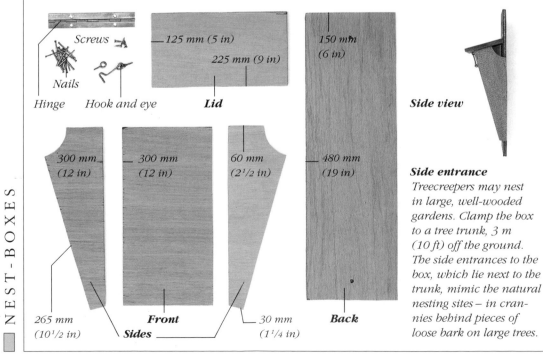

Screws

Nails

Hinge   Hook and eye

125 mm (5 in)

225 mm (9 in)

Lid

150 mm (6 in)

Side view

300 mm (12 in)

300 mm (12 in)

60 mm (2½ in)

480 mm (19 in)

265 mm (10½ in)

Front

Sides

30 mm (1¼ in)

Back

Side entrance
Treecreepers may nest in large, well-wooded gardens. Clamp the box to a tree trunk, 3 m (10 ft) off the ground. The side entrances to the box, which lie next to the trunk, mimic the natural nesting sites – in crannies behind pieces of loose bark on large trees.

• TAWNY OWL BOX •

Side view

The tawny owl does not build a nest and usually lays its eggs in an old tree hole or squirrel's drey. You can tempt a tawny owl to nest in your garden by building this specially designed, chimney-type nest-box or an open-fronted box (p.111) of the same dimensions. (Both types of nest-box may also attract jackdaws.) Cut the base and two sides from a 1.75 m (6 ft) length of 225 x 20 mm (9 x $^3/_4$ in) timber, and the other two pieces (roof and front) from a 550 x 915 mm (2 x 3 ft) sheet of ply, 12 mm ($^1/_2$ in) thick.

Box placement
Nail the batten to the side of a main branch of a tree so that the box lies at an angle of more than 45° to the horizontal. The projecting roof helps to keep the box dry.

Nest lining Spread a thick layer of sawdust or peat over the bottom of the box to absorb the foulings of the nestlings.

Assembly Drill small drainage holes in the base. Using 52 mm (2 in) nails, attach the two thick sides to the base. To complete the box, nail on the front panel and roof.

Fixing the batten
Cut a batten, 700 mm (27$^1/_2$ in) long and 70 mm (2$^3/_4$ in) wide, and drill with holes so that it can be fixed to the box and nailed to the tree. With a bradawl, make pilot holes in the side of the box for screws (as shown in the main photograph).

265 mm (10$^1/_2$ in)

Galvanized nails
52 mm (2 in)

225 mm (9 in)

Base

265 mm (10$^1/_2$ in)

760 mm (30 in)

760 mm (30 in)

225 mm (9 in)

915 mm (36 in)

Front (ply)

Sides

Roof (ply)

Batten

• BIRD-SHELF •

The bird-shelf, which is similar to the open-fronted box (p.111), provides a firm foundation for the nests of spotted fly-catchers, pied wagtails and blackbirds. It is cheap and easy to make and, as the size and shape are not critical, it can be made from scraps of timber. The shelf in the photograph is made from a sheet of plywood, 125 x 770 mm (5 x 30½ in) and 15 mm (⅝ in) thick. Cut out the pieces according to the measurements given.

Front view *The shelf is popular with spotted flycatchers, which like to be able to see out.*

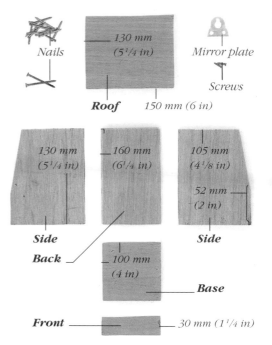

Nails

130 mm (5¼ in)

Mirror plate

Screws

Roof 150 mm (6 in)

130 mm (5¼ in) **Side**

160 mm (6¼ in) **Back**

105 mm (4⅛ in) 52 mm (2 in) **Side**

100 mm (4 in) **Base**

Front 30 mm (1¼ in)

Assembly Use long nails to fix the front and back to the base, and 38 mm (1½ in) ovals for the sides. Attach the roof so that it overhangs at the front. Finally, screw on the mirror plate.

• BOWL-NEST •

House martins build deep cup-shaped nests of mud below a gutter or an eave. They usually nest in colonies at trad-itional sites but you can encourage the birds to adopt a new house by putting up artificial nests. Construct each nest from plaster-of-Paris or quick-drying cement using a 125 mm (5 in) beach ball as a mould. Chalk the outline of the nest on the ball, marking out an entrance hole 60 mm (2½ in) across and 25 mm (1 in) deep. Mould the wet material over the ball to a thickness of 9 mm (⅜ in) and embed a bracket in each side. Next, build a frame from two wooden boards, pro-tected with paint and fixed at right angles. When the bowl-nest is dry, screw it to the frame using the brackets.

Front view *Swallows may also use this man-made nest, sited inside a shed.*

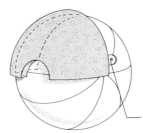

Moulding the nest *Smooth the material with an old, flat knife as it dries. When it is dry, file the edges to fit the frame neatly.*

Bracket *Set brass, right-angled brackets into the material.*

ENCLOSED NEST-BOXES (p.110)

	Floor size	Depth (up to entrance)	Diameter (of entrance hole)	Comments
House sparrow	15 x 15 cm (6 x 6 in)	15 cm (6 in)	32 mm (1¼ in)	Easily disturbed
Jackdaw	20 x 20 cm (7⅞ x 7⅞ in)	40 cm (15¾ in)	150 mm (6 in)	Place in a high, secluded position.
Little owl	120 cm x 20 cm (4 ft x 7⅞ in)	30 cm (12 in)	100 mm (4 in)	Partition the box to darken the hole.
Mallard	30 x 30 cm (12 x 12 in)	20 cm (7⅞ in)	150 mm (6 in)	Position on a raft or island.
Nuthatch	15 x 15 cm (6 x 6 in)	12 cm (4¾ in)	32 mm (1¼ in)	
Starling	15 x 15 cm (6 x 6 in)	30 cm (12 in)	52 mm (2 in)	
Street pigeon	20 x 20 cm (7⅞ x 7⅞ in)	10 cm (4 in)	100 mm (4 in)	Add a perch.
Tits	15 x 12 cm (6 x 4¾ in)	12 cm (4¾ in)	29 mm (1⅛ in)	Great tits also use larger boxes.
Woodpeckers	15 x 15 cm (6 x 6 in)	40 cm (15¾ in)	60 mm (2½ in)	Place high on a trunk.

OPEN-FRONTED NEST BOXES (p.111)

	Floor size	Depth (of box)	Height (to top of front)	Comments
Kestrel	30 x 50 cm (12 x 20 in)	30 cm (12 in)	150 mm (6 in)	Fix on a 5 m (16 ft) pole. Add a perch.
Robin	10 x 10 cm (4 x 4 in)	15 cm (6 in)	52 mm (2 in)	
Wren	10 x 10 cm (4 x 4 in)	15 cm (6 in)	100 mm (4 in)	

BIRD-SHELVES (p.114)

	Floor size	Depth	Height	Comments
Blackbird	20 x 20 cm (7⅞ x 7⅞ in)	20 cm (7⅞ in)	25 mm (1 in)	
Pied wagtail	10 x 10 cm (4 x 4 in)	10 cm (4 in)	25 mm (1 in)	Place in thick cover.
Spotted flycatcher	15 x 15 cm (6 x 6 in)	10 cm (4 in)	25 mm (1 in)	Place with a clear outlook and a perch nearby.

SPECIAL NEST-BOXES

		Comments
House martin	An artificial bowl-nest (p.114)	Fasten under eaves.
Swallow	A bowl-nest (p.114), or half-coconut shell	Site inside shed.
Swift	An oblong-shaped box, 50 x 20 x 10 cm (20 x 7⅞ x 4 in), with an entrance underneath.	Place horizontally beneath eaves.
Tawny owl	A chimney-type box (p.113)	Place under a branch.
Treecreeper	A wedge-shaped box, with a side entrance (p.112)	Mount against a trunk.

CHAPTER FOUR

BEHAVIOUR GUIDE

A BIRD'S CHIEF PRIORITY, like any animal's, is to survive. This means it has to find enough food to fuel the strenuous exercise of flying, to keep warm through cold nights and to build up a reserve of fat against occasional spells of bad weather. Only if it is successful at personal survival can it breed and pass its skills on to the next generation. The different tactics each species employs in the struggle for survival are reflected in the variety of behaviour you are likely to see in the garden. How birds feed, fly, walk, communicate, nest, breed and migrate marks the way they have evolved to make the most of their environment. From the enviable vantage-point of the garden, there is plenty of opportunity to keep watch on the interesting lifestyles of many different types of bird and increase your knowledge of the reasons behind a broad range of activities.

A starling singing and wing-fluttering

∴ THE LIVES OF BIRDS ∴

THE GARDEN BIRDWATCHER ENJOYS observing birds under conditions of comfort and convenience usually denied to the professional ornithologist. You can study birds, often without stepping outdoors, at any hour of the day. We envy birds their freedom, but they also have a routine that, depending on the time of year, may keep them busy from dawn to dusk. In summer, there is the burden of rearing a family while, in winter, survival itself may become a full-time activity.

· THE WAY BIRDS BEHAVE ·

The unequalled opportunity to pry into birds' private lives and habits is a good reason for making the garden an attractive place for birds. Putting out food, providing nest-boxes, planting trees and shrubs, leaving seed heads and even turning a blind eye to insect pests are ways of helping birds survive in an increasingly hostile world, but in the end you make the garden fit for birds so you can enjoy their company. The enjoyment is all the greater if you take the trouble to observe carefully what the birds are doing and appreciate why they are doing it. Appreciation comes in two forms: you can read about a bird's habits and then keep watch in the garden to see them for yourself, or you

Bird study
Tests show that blue tits learn to sip sugar-water, but will ignore pure water from the same apparatus.

Blue tit

can observe something new and refer to books for an explanation. Either way you can derive pleasure from discovering something you did not know before.

We are learning about bird behaviour all the time. It was once difficult to find out about even the most everyday behaviour of garden birds, simply because no-one knew the answers. Some sort of

Bird-table fight *A great tit spreads its wings and displays aggressively to drive a blue tit away from a bird pudding. With a little effort, it has secured the food for itself.*

explanation could be given on the basis that birds seem to do what is sensible and convenient. Scientific research now shows that this is, indeed, the case. At first sight, it seems a spotted flycatcher ought to pursue the largest insects it can find because that way only a few will be needed to satisfy its hunger but, as is described on page 125, butterflies and bees can be so hard to handle that it is more economical of time and energy, and therefore more sensible, to chase smaller insects.

Trying to find the simple advantage for birds in their habits helps to explain much that is going on in the garden, but not every puzzle has been solved and there are still quirks of behaviour that remain unexplained. Why, for instance, do rooks occasionally hang upside-down from telephone wires? Lewis Carroll's young man could ask Old Father William why he stood on his head but you cannot expect an answer from a rook. If you see a rook perched on a wire, you will notice that it sways as if having difficulty balancing. So perhaps it finds hanging upside-down less of a strain than keeping upright.

Much can be learned about bird behaviour simply by keeping careful watch. The hanging terracotta tit-bell outside my window is a great attraction for great and blue tits. They fly in, easily flip upside-down and grab the rim of the tit-bell with their feet, so they can perch while they peck at the appetizing mixture of suet and

nuts that has been set inside. For a long time, house sparrows showed no sign of interest in the tit-bell and I assumed that they did not have the intellectual capacity or flying skill to land on it.

I was wrong. In late winter, one sparrow started to hover under the bell and peck hurriedly at the food before returning to its perch. A few weeks later, several sparrows had learnt the trick and jostled the tits to get at the bell, but they still had to hover, which is like trying to eat while running on the spot. Eventually

The topsy-turvy rook From time to time, rooks hang upside-down: it may be that they find this way up more comfortable.

one sparrow managed to land upside-down and cling to the edge of the bell, like a tit, and feed comfortably. If I had not kept watch for several months, I would have underestimated the intelligence and agility of sparrows.

The hang of it An athletic great tit (above) easily perches on the rim of a terracotta tit-bell. Rather to my surprise, a house sparrow (right), after many attempts, proved itself almost as acrobatic.

· THE DAILY ROUND ·

You will usually notice birds when they are busy: visiting the bird-table; singing from a tree-top; gathering food for their nestlings; or flying overhead to distant feeding-grounds and back to their roosts. The impression is that every moment is run to a tight schedule. Do not overlook the time that birds sometimes spend doing nothing in particular. For part of the year, they may have time to waste.

Sun trap *A young blackbird sunbathes, perhaps because it is well fed and has spare time.*

A long day *Robins get up early and return to the roost late; you may catch sight of one at the bird-table in the fading light.*

During a normal day, a bird has two main activities. It has to feed, which it does in bouts through the day, and it has to maintain its feathers in good condition by preening and bathing. I notice that birds visiting my bird-table are in no hurry to start feeding in the morning. As it becomes light enough to see, birds gather in the trees nearby but they do not begin to feed until it is fully light. Some birds start earlier than others – robins are early risers, while pigeons are late. There is the same staggering of shifts in the evening; gulls and starlings leave early to return to their roosts, while robins are usually the last to disappear. House sparrows extend their working day by catching moths attracted to street lamps.

A bird loses its free time twice in the year. It has to spend more of the day feeding in winter, both because food is in short supply and because extra rations are needed to keep warm. Small birds may have to spend most (if not all) their daylight hours looking for food and the bird-table becomes full of activity. In summer, birds are again busy because they have families to rear. Food is now plentiful but not only do the birds have to feed broods of voracious nestlings, they also have to find additional food to sustain themselves on the day-long chore of journeying to and from the nest.

Pigeon yawning *A woodpigeon relaxes in the safety of an oak tree.*

· THE ANNUAL CYCLE ·

Breeding chore A starling returns to its nest with food for its nestlings. Nesting is a season of severe strain for birds.

Legs extended for landing

midsummer. The tawny owl nests early because it is easier to hunt mice and voles before the grasses grow up and hide them, whereas the sparrowhawk nests late so its offspring are in the nest when there are plenty of young tits and robins about.

After nesting there is a period when birdsong dies down and when birds become less visible. This is the moulting period, when the birds replace worn feathers. The new suit of feathers makes certain that the birds are in peak condition for winter survival or their long migration flights.

Migrant birds are not forced to leave because they cannot find enough food. Preparations for migration start when food is still fairly abundant and reserves of fat can be built up. Departure in autumn is leisurely and will be delayed if the weather holds fine, but in spring the birds are in a hurry to return and start nesting.

There are three main events in the bird's year that are peaks in energy expenditure: breeding, the moult and, for some birds, migration. They do not usually overlap because it is clearly sensible that a bird needs its plumage to be in the best condition when it is migrating or breeding.

Some birds start serious courtship around mid-February but much depends on the weather. Mild winters lead to early courtship and sometimes even egg-laying, but a cold spell will set the programme back and couples split up again. Although egg-laying varies by a few weeks from year to year, a bird's calendar is ultimately organized around gathering food for its young. Egg-laying is timed so that the nestlings grow up when their diet is most plentiful. Tits and robins have young when there are masses of caterpillars. Spotted flycatchers nest nearly two months later because they need the swarms of flying insects that appear in

Early nester A tawny owl broods its young in the rotten wood of a dead tree. Tawny owls nest early in the year, before vegetation grows up and conceals their rodent prey.

∴ FEEDING ∴

N O ANIMAL CAN SURVIVE without the fuel required for growth, for powering muscles and for generating warmth. After finding enough food to keep healthy, a bird has to collect extra food to rear a family. Sufficient amounts are needed to sustain the male through energetic courtship and vigorous defence of territory and the female through the manufacture and incubation of eggs. Later, parents must find food for nestlings.

· WHAT BIRDS EAT ·

Feeding is the most important part of any animal's life. The kind of food that a bird eats and how it eats are the keys to understanding the way it lives. We should avoid judging species by our own standards, condemning starlings, for example, as gluttons for quickly clearing the bird-table or blackbirds as bullies for stealing a thrush's food. Both these habits are natural strategies for obtaining the daily diet. A close look at the feeding habits of garden birds reveals how each one makes a living out of natural food sources; how it adapts its habits to make the best use of supplies; and how you can help it by putting out extra food in birdfeeders.

Looking at the size and shape of a bird's bill provides a good clue to its diet (p.10). Starlings, blackbirds and gulls have "general purpose" bills that enable them to take advantage of a wide variety of foods and that have led to their abundance in towns and the countryside. Other birds have bills shaped for specific purposes that limit the types of food they can eat. Finches, for example, generally have conical bills for cracking seeds, but even among garden finches there are differences in bill size and shape that are reflected in their choices of food.

The goldfinch and the siskin are particularly adept at probing deep into the heads of thistles to extract seeds because of their slender bills. Other finches have to tear open the seed heads or wait for the seeds to become loose.

Hawthorn berries
– winter food

Specialized bills *The goldfinch (left) has a tweezer-like bill for picking seeds from teazels and thistles whereas the bullfinch's strong, broad bill (above) crushes seeds and fruits.*

The greenfinch, with its short, broad bill, eats the large, exposed seeds of cereals, elm, bramble, groundsel and burdock. It often picks fallen seeds from the ground. The hawfinch, which you can often overlook in gardens because of its retiring nature, has a large bill with powerful jaw muscles that can crack the stones of cherries and sloes, but it also eats seeds of elms and other trees.

The bullfinch has a short, sharp-edged bill that is used effectively for plucking buds, deftly crushing and peeling seeds and fruits and even shelling small snails. However, it finds picking up loose seeds difficult. In contrast, the chaffinch and brambling have long bills for pecking at seeds on the ground but they are unable to deal with seed heads.

Foothold A kestrel grips a mouse in its sharp talons to eat it.

However, none of the finches has a more specialized bill than the large, odd-looking crossbill. Although the uniquely shaped bill (the ends of which curve and cross over) is custom-built for extracting seeds from cones, the design does not restrict the crossbill to a diet of conifer seeds. The bill can also be used to split open apples and remove the pips inside, or to prise bark off tree trunks and expose insects hiding underneath. The case of the crossbill shows that, within limits, bills do allow birds to be somewhat adaptable in their feeding behaviour.

The bill of a bird is a versatile organ used with amazing dexterity both in feeding and nest-building, but only a few species use the feet to hold food when eating. The bullfinch husks seeds by the co-ordinated use of its tongue and the two halves of its bill; it never

Crossbill A uniquely shaped bill enables the uncommon crossbill to extract seeds from pine, larch and spruce cones.

Pine cones – opened by crossbills

uses its feet to hold seeds. On the other hand, the goldfinch regularly uses a foot to hold birch or alder catkins while pecking at them. Birds of prey, such as sparrowhawks and kestrels, pounce on small mammals with their talons to kill them and hold on to their catch when feeding. Tits and crows use their feet and, by using their bills and feet together, will even learn to pull up a string to eat food, such as peanuts in their shells, attached to the other end.

Overstretched A coal tit demonstrates its acrobatic skills as it tries to stabilize a swinging peanut feeder.

· ECONOMICAL FEEDING ·

Putting yourself in the position of a bird trying to feed economically is a useful means of understanding the way it behaves. Within the limits of its bill size, toe structure and other physical characteristics, as well as its acrobatic and aerobatic

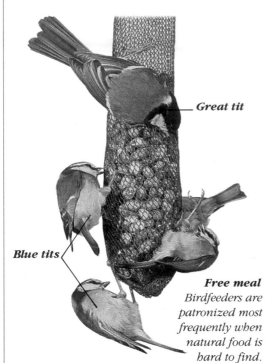

— **Great tit**

Blue tits

Free meal
Birdfeeders are patronized most frequently when natural food is hard to find.

abilities, a bird chooses the best food available. As a rule, birds behave sensibly and try to get the most nutrition for the least effort. Their objective is clear when expressed in financial terms: a bird's aim in life is to make a good living, earning the best income (food) for the least expenditure (energy spent getting the food). A healthy surplus, which is stored as fat, creates a reserve for a rainy day and the capital to spend on events like breeding and migration. Bird-tables are popular because they provide an easier living than searching for natural foods.

Within the broad range of its diet, a bird selects the food that is easiest to obtain. Bullfinches prefer the seeds of

ash, bramble, dock or nettle. Only when these crops are exhausted towards the end of winter will you see them descending upon orchards and devastating the fruit trees by pecking off 30 or more buds per minute. The time the bullfinch spends on this destructive activity depends on how much other food it can find. The fruit-grower curses the bullfinch, but stripping buds is its last resort. Buds contain so little sustenance that a bullfinch has to consume large numbers of them just to stay alive.

You are most likely to see odd feeding habits when the staple diet is in short supply. For instance, if desperately hungry, fieldfares will attack turnips and, during dry spells, blackbirds feed their nestlings on crusts of white bread because they cannot find worms. Similarly, song thrushes usually open snails only as an emergency ration in times of frost or drought because smashing shells requires a lot of effort. The operation becomes even more tedious when blackbirds spot an easy meal and steal the results of the song thrush's hard work.

The flexible rules of bird economics are best demonstrated by the spotted flycatcher when hawking above a garden lawn. It waits on a perch and flies out in sorties to catch insects on the wing. As it

Expensive meal *The time and energy spent swinging a large snail repeatedly against a stone anvil means snail meat is an expensive food for a song thrush.*

depletes the insects within range of one perch, the flycatcher moves to the next and works its way around the garden.

When insects are in abundance the flycatcher's preference is for nourishing flies of bluebottle size, because they are easily caught and easily swallowed. But-terflies and bees are ignored – although they make a larger meal, they take more time to deal with. At the other end of the scale, tiny midges and mosquitoes are swallowed without trouble but a lot of energy-consuming trips are needed to gather enough for a satisfying meal.

The flycatcher will switch to different prey if circumstances change. When it comes across lots of butterflies feeding on buddleias, it picks them off with ease or, if it finds a swarm of midges, it quickly snaps up several of them before returning to its perch. In both instances, it is seizing the opportunity of an effortless meal.

Bite size food
Spotted flycatchers prefer flying insects of bluebottle size, such as this big-headed fly, but will take whatever is readily available.

· HOARDING ·

One way to avoid going hungry is to save some food when there is a surplus, like depositing hard-earned money in a bank. Sometimes you may find peanuts and sunflower seeds disappearing from the bird-table more quickly than you would expect from the number of birds feeding on it. This is because some birds are carrying them away to hide. The coal tit, marsh tit and nuthatch are common hoarders and carry off fragments of peanuts from the birdfeeder to wedge in crevices in rough bark. (They often take the food so far away that you cannot see where it is hidden.) Food is hoarded when it is abundant, as in autumn or at a birdfeeder. Nuts are frequently hidden because they are nutritious and keep well, but tits also store insects, and members of the crow family bury bread, meat and other scraps. Hidden food may be left for weeks before the owner returns to claim it. The bird apparently remembers the

exact location by reference to nearby landmarks. Jays can even recover buried acorns from under a deep layer of snow.

Hoards are a useful emergency store against temporary hard times, but the two nutcracker species of northern Europe and America depend on hazelnuts stored in autumn for winter survival and for raising their young in spring.

Future needs *A coal tit, a common hoarder, carries a peanut from a hanging basket to hide for later consumption.*

• NEW FOODS •

Studies of garden birds have proved valuable in showing how birds learn to take new foods. It is usual for one or two starlings or house sparrows in the garden to learn to obtain food, like the tits, from a peanut bag or tit-bell (p.119), but it is hard to tell whether they mastered this skill by a flash of inspiration or by copying the tits at work. Birds normally discover what to eat by trial-and-error. The

Occasionally the behaviour is genuinely new. The most famous example is tits learning to steal cream by poking their bills through the tops of milk bottles. When deliveries of milk in bottles, sealed with cardboard or foil tops, became widespread, blue and great tits added this nourishing food to their diet. (Even the great spotted woodpecker has been seen feeding on milk in this way.) It seems that the habit started in several places independently but rapidly spread as more birds learnt the trick. The bottles are opened by the same technique tits employ to hammer open nuts or prise bark off trees in search of insects. It is possible that the birds that originally pioneered the habit accidentally found the milk as they probed in search of natural food.

Red patch under tail

New food source Great spotted woodpeckers regularly eat seeds and nuts but visiting birdfeeders is a relatively new habit.

selection of seeds by different finches is a result of young birds trying all sorts of seeds and returning to those they can deal with efficiently with their size and shape of bill. Young blackbirds peck at everything to learn what is edible. The learning process may be speeded up by watching and imitating parents or other members of the flock.

Sometimes a new habit crops up and you see birds behaving in an unusual fashion. The great spotted woodpecker hunts for insects in typical woodpecker fashion, chiselling wood to expose insects hiding within, but there are records of woodpeckers swooping like a flycatcher at flying insects. Unusual behaviour may be due to birds learning a new trick, or it could be a regular (but rare) part of the species' instinctive repertoire.

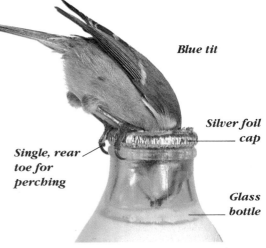

Blue tit

Silver foil cap

Single, rear toe for perching

Glass bottle

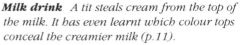

Milk drink A tit steals cream from the top of the milk. It has even learnt which colour tops conceal the creamier milk (p.11).

· BIRDS AND FRUIT ·

It is easy to become upset when birds strip your carefully nurtured crop of fruit as soon as it begins to ripen, but from the plants' point of view, the birds are doing them a favour. Fruit is the plants' method of getting their seeds distributed. Some plants have seeds that are borne by the wind, like the downy seeds of thistles and the keys of sycamore and ash, but fleshy fruits are designed to be eaten. The

qualities that attract birds – bright colours (often red or yellow) that contrast with the surrounding green foliage, and a sweet, juicy package of flesh – are the same as those that attract us. Once swallowed, the flesh of the fruit is digested but the seeds are deposited far from the parent plant. Mistletoe is well known for being spread by birds.

The flesh of fruit is not as nutritious as a diet of insects or seeds but its advantage is that it is easier to gather. Fruit is important food for many birds in winter, especially during severe weather, and it may be vital again during periods of summer drought. In winter, a bird can save a lot of energy if it can find a fruit tree and gorge itself, then perch quietly nearby, feathers fluffed out, until the next meal is due.

The chief garden birds that regularly eat fruit and disperse their seeds are thrushes, some warblers (such as blackcaps and garden warblers), starlings and members of the crow family. Other species, including finches, tits and woodpigeons, eat the seeds as well as the flesh, upsetting the mutually beneficial relationship between plants and birds. Nevertheless, tits and woodpigeons do sometimes disperse seeds.

Fruit-eaters often feed in flocks and one of the delightful sights of winter is to see a crowd of blackbirds or fieldfares at work in a holly tree or dotted along a hawthorn hedge. Sometimes a mistle thrush or fieldfare attempts to defend its private fruit tree against all comers. The effort is worthwhile because the bird stands to keep its secure food supply, but it may be overwhelmed if a flock of fruit-eaters invades. Then the erstwhile owner has no option but to join them in stripping the tree of its fruit as fast as possible.

Old fruit *In winter, an old, rotten apple left on the lawn provides a large and easy meal for the mistle thrush.*

Red fruits *Birds seem especially attracted to bright red berries.*

Spindle

Holly

Honeysuckle

∴ FLIGHT PATTERNS ∴

THE POWER OF FLIGHT gives birds opportunities for easy movement denied to all other animals except insects and bats. Squirrels, dormice and wood mice climb trees to feed and nest but they cannot flit from tree to tree or twig to twig like a bird. Badgers and deer travel from their resting-places in search of food but they do not range as far as a starling or heron.

· THE COST OF FLIGHT ·

While the great advantage of flight is speed, the drawback is that it uses large amounts of energy – 10–15 times as much as walking. It is quicker to fly in a jet aeroplane than to go by car but it is more expensive. Like the human traveller, a bird must sometimes decide whether to forgo speed in the interest of economy. When you throw stale bread out of the kitchen window, a starling at the bottom of the garden must decide whether to run across the lawn or fly. Flight is worth the extra effort if the starling has to beat its greedy companions to the food.

Some birds, as different as wrens and mallards, have to keep flapping to stay in the air, but many birds

reduce the cost of flight by gliding effortlessly. Gulls flap regularly when flying directly from their roosts to feed on refuse tips, but glide in slow, energy-saving circles once they arrive, so they can scan the ground for food. They also soar gracefully above gardens on gusts of wind billowing around buildings. Swifts use this effect to double advantage. Rolling eddies

Insect trap Swifts sometimes seize the opportunity of feeding on insects caught up in eddies (miniature whirlwinds).

of air, created along a line of trees by a stiff breeze, collect swarms of insects. The swifts abandon their usual headlong careering around the sky to gather in the eddy; they fly slowly forward into the wind, almost hovering at times, to snap up the rich crop of insects trapped by the spinning air currents. Swifts also use *thermals* – the updraughts of air that rise through the atmosphere when the ground warms up on a sunny day. Thermals are another form of insect trap and swifts, joined perhaps by some

Short, rounded wings

Sleek, aerodynamic body

Wren in flight *Wrens fly rapidly and directly; the continuous flapping of their wings makes a noticeable whirring sound.*

swallows, martins, gulls or starlings, allow themselves to drift upwards while they enjoy an effortless meal.

Over long distances, economy can be more important than speed. Rooks soar in thermals as an energy-saving means of travel. Small birds cannot use thermals but some, like tits, finches and starlings, save energy with a bounding flight, in which they alternately flap and close their wings. This gives the typical bouncing effect of a flock of finches. They close their wings rather than glide because, for birds of this size, the disadvantage of drag on the outstretched wings outweighs the advantage of the lift they generate.

Energetic flapping

Caterpillar

Blue tit

Closed wings

Bounding flight
Flapping carries a blue tit upwards, when it closes its wings it hurtles through the air before dropping.

Closed wings

Flapping

CRUISING FLIGHT SPEEDS
Figures are in miles per hour.

Blue tit	18	Sparrowhawk	27
Carrion crow	31	Starling	21
Heron	27	Swallow	20
Herring gull	25	Swift	25
Mallard	40	Woodpigeon	38
Pheasant	34	Wren	20

·TAKE-OFF AND LANDING·

Like an aeroplane, a bird has to achieve a minimum speed to become airborne. To generate lift the wings are swept to and fro to create an airflow over them. As with an aeroplane, take-off and landing are easier into the wind because it gives extra lift. Most garden birds take off by leaping into the air; for a split-second they are hovering just clear of the ground. This is strenuous, but the leap helps the bird with an extra "shove" upwards. You can often hear pigeons, which are heavy-bodied birds, take off with a loud whipcrack. This is the sound of their

Footprints *The swift departure of a black-bird is recorded in the soft snow. You can see the marks made by its wing tips and the deep imprint of its feet as it leapt into the air.*

Kick start
A juvenile male kestrel launches itself upwards with a shove.

Touchdown *In order to catch prey, a tawny owl must land with precision. The spread wings and fanned tail give the owl control and stability as it slows down.*

wings being flung forwards and down to start air moving over the flight surfaces. Larger birds cannot generate enough power to hover so they simply drop off a perch, spread their wings and accelerate with gravity or, when on the ground, run a few steps to take off. It is more difficult to leap off water: ducks manage but coots and swans have to run to get airborne.

Landing is the opposite of take-off. The bird has to lose as much speed as possible without falling out of the air. Small birds slow down easily, until they are virtually hovering on rapidly whirring wings, and then gently touch down. Large birds have to be more careful. When landing on a perch, they swoop below it and then climb to lose speed. They land on the ground with a thump and run for a short distance to lose momentum, or hit water with a splash, sliding to a standstill.

· WINGS AND TAILS ·

The size and shape of a bird's wings determine the way it flies. In essence, broad wings give good lift for slow flight, like that of a wheeling rook, or rapid, vertical take-off, like that of the pheasant when it explodes into the sky. Tails give manoeuvrability – a bird can still fly when it has lost its tail-feathers but it is handicapped. However, there is no obvious explanation for the excessively long tails of certain species, such as magpies, long-tailed tits and pheasants.

You can learn a lot about a bird's way of life from the general shape of its wings and tail. A variety of wing designs has

evolved, each suited to a specific diet and lifestyle. For example, whereas the swift hunts for flying insects by speeding through the air and alternating bursts of flickering wing beats with short glides, the

Lift-off *A street pigeon takes off. On the upstroke, the flight-feathers separate and act as extra aerofoils.*

Rook *Long, broad wings and a round tail create good lift, enabling the rook to glide with little effort while looking for food on the ground.*

White rump

Tail fanned *– a flap for extra lift*

swallow often flies near the ground or over water with a less economical, flapping flight. Yet the swallow is the more efficient hunter because its longer tail makes it more manoeuvrable and enables it to pursue and catch larger and faster insects. This explains why swallows arrive in Europe before swifts, depart for Africa after them and rear more young during the breeding season.

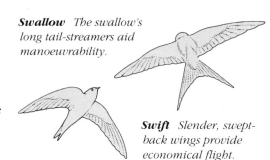

Swallow The swallow's long tail-streamers aid manoeuvrability.

Swift Slender, swept-back wings provide economical flight.

·HOVERING·

Part of the lift generated by the wings comes from their flapping action and part comes from the flow of air over them caused by the bird's forward movement. The slower a bird flies, the less lift that is generated by the air flow and it has to flap harder. When a bird is hovering it relies almost entirely on lift created by flapping, which consumes a large amount of energy. The kestrel is one of the few birds to hover regularly but other species hover when the occasion demands – for example, to pick insects from leaves or seize growing fruit. Blackbirds, robins, chaffinches and starlings are not agile enough to land upside-down on a tit-bell like the tits, but they can hover long enough underneath one to stab several times at the mixture of fat and scraps inside. Even rooks can manage a clumsy hover to eat food they cannot otherwise reach.

Hovering kestrel In effect, the kestrel flies forward into the wind at the same speed as it is being blown back, so its speed relative to the ground remains zero.

On the outside A great tit, fooled by the transparent perspex of the feeder, hovers in a vain attempt to obtain a peanut.

RSPB space feeder

·FORMATION FLYING·

It seems amazing that there are not more collisions as a gang of house sparrows takes to the air when disturbed, or as a tightly packed flock of starlings circles in the fading light before going to roost. A flock shows marvellous communal co-ordination when taking off, and changes direction like a single bird. The secret is that birds are alert to the slightest movements of others. As one bird crouches and begins to spread its wings before take-off, the others quickly follow suit and leap into the air almost simultaneously. Similarly, the flock wheels in precision when one or two birds decide to alter course, and a wave of movement passes along the mass of birds. Each bird watches not its immediate neighbour but several birds in front and times its maneouvre as the wave of movement reaches it.

∵ PERCHING AND WALKING ∴

THE BODIES OF BIRDS are superbly adapted for flight, but most birds spend only a small part of their lives in the air. In the garden, you are more likely to see birds perched on a tree or shrub, hopping across a lawn or climbing among foliage in search of food. The feet of birds, like their wings, vary between different species according to each species' needs.

• PERCHING •

Most garden birds belong to the large group of species (p.188) called the *Passeriformes* or *passerines* (literally, sparrow-like birds). Many birds, including some seabirds, regularly perch, but the feet of passerines are most suited to grasping twigs and wires. Some, like the tits and warblers, are very acrobatic.

Grip *A sparrow's toes clamp around a perch.*

A perching bird's foot has four toes – three in front and one behind. The rear toe is short on walking birds, such as chickens, and on swimming birds, such as ducks. Perching birds have a much longer rear toe that is opposable (like a thumb) and gives a firm grip on a slender twig. When landing on a vertical surface, long, needle-sharp claws help maintain a strong hold, as tits demonstrate on bird-tables.

Sleeping on a perch would be a precarious business except that perching birds are able to "lock" on to the perch so that their grip will not relax as they doze off. The tendons that flex the toes run around the ankle and knee joints. As the bird's weight settles on landing and the leg bends, these tendons are pulled and they automatically bend the toes around the perch. The toes only uncurl as a bird takes off – when its weight is removed and its legs straighten. A second locking-device operates on the underside of each tendon in the toe. When a bird perches, hundreds of tiny knobs press between ribs on a surrounding tendon-sheath.

• CLIMBING •

Most specialized tree-climbers tend to have short legs with strong toes that make clinging to a vertical surface easy. The woodpeckers, which are the most specialized, have a different arrangement of toes: two facing forwards and two backwards.

They also have specially stiffened tail-feathers with which they brace themselves against trunks. The treecreeper is similarly endowed and both these birds hop up trunks and out along branches, sometimes underneath, in their search for food. After examining one tree, they fly down to the base of the next and work their way up again. The nuthatch, by contrast, does not use its short tail as a prop and can go up and down trees with equal ease. The use of the tail as a prop is not confined to woodpeckers and treecreepers. You can see tits support themselves with their tails when they land on upright feeders, and starlings and sparrows do so when they alight at nest-boxes. Magpies have also been seen using their long tails to climb tree trunks like the woodpeckers.

Hunting *A great spotted woodpecker inspects a hole in a tree for beetle larvae.*

Two backward-facing toes

Tail – *used as a prop*

·HOPPING AND WALKING·

Generally, birds that spend much of their time in trees, especially the smaller birds, hop when on the ground. This seems to be because hopping is the best way of moving through trees, jumping from perch to perch. Birds that spend more time on the ground either walk or run. Thus chaffinches walk but greenfinches, which less frequently feed on the ground, hop. The exceptions include the ground-dwelling dunnock, which hops, and the blackbird, which both hops and walks.

Walker *The coot (left), like other water birds, walks. It has a rather awkward gait.*

On the hop *The blue tit (right) is typical of many small, tree-dwelling birds in that it hops on the ground.*

·HEAD-NODDING·

From peacocks in stately homes and chickens in the run to pigeons, starlings and wagtails on the lawn, nodding the head to and fro is common among birds that walk rather than hop. You might think a nodding bird would find it hard to see where it was going, let alone find food. (Try reading this while swinging your head from side to side.) Yet if you could see the movement in slow motion, the true state of affairs would be revealed. At every step, there is a point where, although the head is moving relative to the body, it is stationary compared to its surroundings. This keeps the eyes steady and makes it easier to pick out tiny morsels of food or distant predators. (Birds that hop take advantage of the pause between each jump to scrutinize their neighbourhood.) The evidence that head-nodding is a means of fixing the eyes comes from an experiment in which pigeons had to walk on a moving conveyor-belt. When the speed was adjusted so that the pigeons were stationary relative to their surroundings, they stopped nodding.

∴ CARE AND MAINTENANCE ∴

A BIRD'S FEATHERS PERFORM two main functions: they keep the bird warm and dry and provide the lift and control surfaces for flight. When feathers are damaged or lost, the layer of insulation is impaired, and flight becomes more strenuous. This inefficiency could cost birds their lives in severe weather or if they are pursued by a predator, so it is vital that plumage is kept in top condition by daily care and attention, and that wear and tear is put right, once or twice a year, by moulting.

• PREENING •

The secret of a feather's strength and flexibility lies in its thousands of barbs, which are linked together by hooked barbules like a zip fastener. Air trapped between these barbs gives the feather its insulating and waterproof qualities. Some of these barbs become unzipped by daily wear and have to be repaired by preening.

Zipping up
A barn owl runs a vane through its bill.

Preening consists of gently nibbling or stroking the feathers one at a time with the closed bill so that splits between the barbs are zipped up. You can simulate the effects of preening with any feather. A gentle pull splits the vane by unhooking neighbouring rows of barbules. Match the two edges together again and run the join firmly between thumb and forefinger and it will zip up again. The nibbling and rubbing also remove dirt and parasites (such as feather lice and mites) and arrange feathers back into position.

At intervals during preening, the bird squeezes its bill against the preen gland under its tail to collect preen oil, which it spreads in a thin film over the feathers. The precise function of this oil is not known but it appears to kill bacteria and fungi. You can tell if a bird has been prevented from oiling by its scruffy plumage.

Wear and tear
A close-up of the edge of a feather vane (right) shows how two of its interlocking barbs develop a split once the barbules become unhooked. Gentle, precise nibbles with the bill fit the barbs into position.

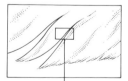

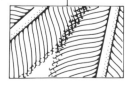

Those parts of the bird's body that cannot be reached directly by the bill, such as the head, are preened by scratching with the feet. Preen oil is transferred either by scratching the oil-laden bill before scratching the head (p.9), or by rubbing the head against previously oiled feathers.

Keeping clean *While a little casual preening is done at odd moments, the mallard, like all other birds, sets aside time to clean and rearrange its feathers in a systematic preen.*

· BATHING ·

Most garden birds bathe and the importance of a regular bath to keep the plumage in top condition is shown by the number of birds that come to the birdbath as soon as you clear the ice on a frosty morning. Starlings have even been seen breaking the ice for themselves.

Drying off *A song thrush rapidly flaps its wings and shakes its tail to throw off excess water.*

After checking that it is not going to be caught unawares by a cat, the bird enters the shallow water. It ruffles its feathers and wets them by ducking into the water or by shaking its head from side to side, while rolling its body and flicking water with its wings. Next, it squats to immerse

Water wings *Crouching low in a bird-bath, a robin uses its wings and fanned tail to splash water on to its back.*

its belly and scoops water over its back with its wings. Raising and lowering the feathers allows water to wash the skin. The bird is careful not to get so waterlogged that it cannot escape an attack.

Afterwards, the bedraggled bird flies to a safe perch to dry off. It shakes its wings and tail to remove much of the water. Ruffling the body-feathers lets the air circulate and helps dry the plumage and settle it into place. A preen provides the final polish and rearrangement.

As an alternative to the bird-bath, pigeons take showers in the rain. They lean over, place one wing in the air and raise their body-feathers to let water run in. Warblers and some other birds bathe by flying through rain-soaked foliage. Swallows, swifts and even owls momentarily dip into pools of water while in flight.

Ornithologists are not decided on the exact function of bathing. Cleaning the feathers does not appear to be the main purpose. It is possible that preen oil spreads more easily over damp feathers. Experiments have shown that feathers become more flexible when wet, so bathing could be a means of restoring feathers to their proper shape.

Birds even have a form of dry-cleaning. The house sparrow, among garden birds, indulges in *dust-bathing*, which usually follows water-bathing. It lands in the loose, dry soil of a flowerbed or on a dusty path and goes through the same motions as in water-bathing. Several other sparrows may join in and squabbles will break out if they interfere with each other's exuberant actions. When they fly off to preen, a crater is left in the soil.

• SUNBATHING •

We sunbathe because of the pleasant sensation of hot sun on our bare skin or to work on our tans but it is not so clear why birds choose to bask in the sun. Sometimes they simply perch in a sun-trap to keep warm on a cool day; black-birds sunbathe with their wings spread on the snow in severely cold but clear weather so they may be trying to absorb the weak rays of the sun. However, this cannot be the whole explanation because birds also choose to bask in the full heat of the sun on a hot summer day. They often "pant" with the bill open so they must be trying to keep cool.

Places in the sun A collared dove (left) *enjoys high-intensity sunbathing. Sunbathing is not simply a matter of keeping warm; the* blackbird (above) *suggests that it is already hot enough by panting with its bill open.*

From the way birds seem to be almost in a trance, wearing a rather vacant expression, it could be argued that they are just enjoying themselves as much as human sun-addicts, but the true function of sun-bathing is probably to assist feather maintenance. It has been shown that a vulture's feathers that have become twisted during flight straighten out with a few minutes' exposure to the sun but take several hours to repair in the shade. There could be a similar process at work in the feathers of our garden birds.

· MOULT ·

Despite daily maintenance, the plumage eventually becomes worn from the stresses of flight and constant friction against foliage and the nest. The bird becomes scruffy, so, at least once a year, it sheds its worn feathers and replaces them with a new set. To minimize the disruption to the bird's life, plumage is replaced gradually: as old feathers fall out, new ones sprout in their place so that there are no large gaps. Small song-birds take about five weeks to moult and starlings take about three months.

The only obvious gaps in plumage are in the long feathers of the wings and, to a lesser extent, the tail. You can see the gaps in the wings of crows and rooks as they fly overhead in winter because their flight-feathers are shed slowly so that they are never deprived of too many at once.

The moult is a time of strain. Not only does a bird with an incomplete plumage have to use more energy keeping warm and flying, but it has to find extra energy for manufacturing new feathers. Moulting birds become retiring, saving their energy by perching quietly and keeping out of the way of predators, which can now catch them more easily. Most birds moult at the end of the breeding season but some have another moult before nesting. Both moults take place when the birds are free of the strain of rearing their families and when food is still abundant. The new plumage gives them a better chance of surviving winter weather or the strain of a long migration flight. One exception to this rule is the swift, which moults after it has returned to Africa.

The gradual abrasion of individual feathers is used by some birds to change colour. After the summer moult, the male brambling is a rather undistinguished bird with a brown head and back but, over the course of winter, the buff tips to the feathers wear away to reveal the glossy black of the breeding plumage.

Damaged feathers
You can see the wear on feathers that have naturally dropped off a bird: the colours are dull, the edges frayed and the vane is threadbare and generally untidy.

New suit of feathers
The white spots that make the fresh autumn plumage of the starling so striking are worn away as the starling squeezes in and out of its nest hole.

Abnormal moult   This magpie has lost all its head-feathers at once. The new feathers are sprouting from waxy sheaths.

∵ ROOSTING AND SLEEPING ∵

BIRDS ARE MOSTLY CREATURES of the day, although owls and often ducks feed at night and roost during the day. Garden birds, especially, retire to roost as darkness falls and become active again before it is light enough for you to see them. Roosting time differs between species – large-eyed robins are still searching for worms after sparrows and pigeons have retired for the night. In the garden you can detect roosting sites by looking out for the accumulation of droppings underneath.

· ROOSTING ·

Regular roosting places must give protection from predators and shelter from the elements. A hole in a tree, or a nest-box, is the best place on both counts but even a bare tree gives some protection from the wind. A study showed that a leafless thicket slowed down the wind speed sufficiently for roosting blackbirds to save a third or more of the fat that they would otherwise have used to keep warm.

The nest is often used as a roost, especially by the female before laying her eggs, but a few birds make special roosts for the winter. In regions where the winters are severe, but rarely in Britain, house sparrows build winter nests, smaller than breeding nests and well-lined with feathers. Similarly, woodpeckers may

drill out special holes in winter and treecreepers sometimes scoop out circular niches in rotten wood or the thick, spongy bark of Wellingtonia trees. The shelter of a roost increases if birds huddle together for warmth. In winter, wrens gather in nest-boxes and family parties of long-tailed tits line up on branches, unlike other tits which roost alone in holes.

Blackbirds will roost in their territories, providing there is a suitable site. If your garden is without sheltering bushes, you

Winter roost
White droppings on a Wellingtonia mark a treecreeper roost.

Communal roost *Street pigeons enjoy a final preen before settling down to sleep in a willow tree.*

may lose the blackbirds in the evening, especially in winter, as they fly away to roost, preferably in a clump of evergreens. Hundreds have been known to meet at a single site. Finches, pigeons, gulls and house sparrows also practise mass roosting, while starlings are famous for their huge roosts that become such a nuisance in city centres. The regular evening migration of birds to their roosts, whether strung-out Vs of gulls or mobs of starlings, is a familiar urban sight. Small parties set out from the feeding-grounds, gather at traditional staging-posts, and arrive at the roost in a swarm.

Communal roosts give the same safety in numbers as a daytime flock (p.140) and may also be a means of finding a good place to feed. A hungry bird follows well-fed companions when they leave the roost in the morning because they will return to where they found food before.

• SLEEPING •

Few birds sleep with their "heads tucked under their wings": that would be an awkward posture. The bill is tucked under the *scapular* (shoulder) feathers or the head is drawn into the breast. The feathers are fluffed out to keep warm and one leg is often brought up to the body. Swifts are believed to slumber on the wing (they also roost in their nests) and moorhens "cat-nap" while swimming in circles.

It is very difficult to creep up unobserved on a sleeping bird. You can see this is the case when watching a group of

Sitting duck *A female mallard* (right) *sleeps during the day. She will take turns with others to keep guard and prevent an ambush.*

Blanket of feathers *A hen chaffinch retains body heat while asleep by fluffing out her feathers to trap a thick, insulating layer of air.*

sleeping pigeons or mallards. You will notice that each bird opens its eyes at regular intervals. This is a necessary precaution against surprise attacks from predators. As you get nearer, the birds will open their eyes more frequently to keep a careful watch on your movements.

The precise function of sleep is still something of a mystery, even in humans. The best explanation is that sleep is the most effective means for a bird to save energy when it has time to spare. Some birds are known to lower their body temperature during sleep and therefore save more energy. Because a resting bird is immobile and quiet, it also seems likely that sleep helps to make the bird less of a conspicuous target for passing predators. Whatever the case, sleeping in a safe, sheltered roost is a great advantage.

·: FLOCKS :·

SOME BIRDS LIVE IN flocks while you see others only in ones or twos. Starlings, for example, are gregarious, while robins are solitary, although they sometimes gather to spend winter nights in communal roosts. There are sensible reasons why some birds choose to live in flocks and others prefer the single life.

· THE BENEFITS OF FLOCKS ·

A bird in a flock gets protection from predators simply because a hawk, say, finds it difficult to concentrate its swooping attack on a single target if there is a number of birds milling about. Imagine trying to catch a tennis ball when you have dropped a whole box of them: it is hard to pick one from the half-dozen bouncing all over the place. In addition, the hawk knows that it could hurt itself by colliding with one of the flock, so you will see starlings bunch into a tight formation if a hawk appears. There is safety in numbers: each starling selfishly makes use of its companions because there is less chance of it being singled out by a predator if it is in a flock.

Birds in a flock also stand a better chance in the event of an attack because many pairs of eyes are better for keeping watch. Careful experiments have proved

that flocks take off sooner than single birds when danger threatens. Even though the difference is measured in fractions of a second, it may be enough time to secure an escape.

As a result, a bird does not need to spend as much time scanning its surroundings for danger when it is part of a flock. You will notice that a bird on your bird-table stops eating at frequent intervals to cock its head and look around. If it is joined by other birds it can afford to be less vigilant and, by relying on the others to share guard duty, can increase the time it spends feeding.

The second major advantage of flocking is that it helps birds find food. To save time searching for food, birds watch others to see what they find. After one or two starlings arrive at your birdfeeder, a horde quickly descends. When the first

V-formation *Each winter evening, black-headed gulls* (above) *return to their roosts.*

Warning *Starlings* (left) *rely on each other to keep guard.*

bird swooped into the garden, the others realized that it had found a source of food and rushed to join it.

With birds paying attention to the activities of others, word soon gets around that you are putting out pieces of food, and birds will flock into your garden. Then, if the supply dries up, the disappointed visitors will look elsewhere, perhaps by following flock mates who appear to know where to go.

Following others also operates at a local level when birds are feeding. In winter, flocks of tits, joined by goldcrests

haws; and goldfinches on waste ground covered with seeding groundsel. These patches are spaced out and the difficult part is to find one, therefore many eyes make light work. Other kinds of food, however, are thinly but evenly spread. In these circumstances, birds in a flock only get in each other's way and it is better to hunt alone, concentrating in one area and getting to know where the best places are to search. When necessary, this hunting-ground will be defended against rivals, as it is with robins and tawny owls in their winter territories.

Communal feeding Rooks (left) *nest near one another and eat together. It is in the best interest of birds like street pigeons* (above) *to feed together when exposed on open ground.*

and treecreepers, feed on tiny insects and even smaller insect eggs on leaves or lodged in crevices. Such food must be hard to find, even by sharp-eyed birds, so time is saved by watching each others' efforts. If one tit finds aphids skulking in the foliage, the other birds will search leaves. When another finds rich pickings of dormant caterpillars or pupae, the flock will start to look for this new food.

So, why do not all birds live in flocks if they provide such advantages? A solitary lifestyle has its compensations. Avoiding predators can be achieved by slipping into cover or relying on stealth and camouflage, when it makes more sense to be alone. Feeding in a group is only an advantage if there is plenty of food. Flocking birds specialize in feeding on large patches of food: pigeons descend on brassicas; fieldfares alight on hedges thick with

Nut basket

Blue tits

Three's company
Communal feeding is worthwhile only where there is enough food, as at a birdfeeder.

141

∴ SPACE AND TERRITORY ∴

A LL BIRDS KEEP a clear personal space around themselves. The size of this space varies according to the bird's particular lifestyle, social position and circumstances. It is sensible policy for a bird to keep its distance from its neighbour. It stops collisions when a flock takes to the air and prevents conflict when feeding. Birds also defend a fixed area called a *territory*, which is needed for feeding or breeding or both.

• INDIVIDUAL DISTANCE •

If two birds come too close to each other, one will give way. The minimum distance at which they still accept one another is called the *individual distance*. You can see the limit when swallows space themselves out along telephone wires. Birds keep out of each other's reach, so individual distance depends on the size of the species. It is about 30 cm (12 in) for black-headed gulls and less for smaller

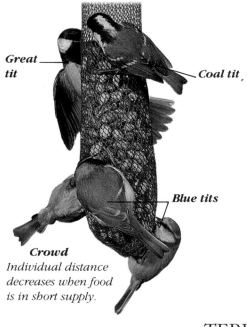

Great tit

Coal tit

Blue tits

Crowd
Individual distance decreases when food is in short supply.

Keep away *A black-headed gull displays a "forward threat" to keep intruders from its space.*

birds. The amount of personal space also depends on circumstances: it is zero between mates or birds that roost together. Individual distances stop birds squabbling or getting in each other's way. Starlings space apart on the lawn to creep up on worms: another starling trampling nearby causes worms to hide in their burrows.

Conflicts of interest over perches and food are settled quickly because each bird knows its rank in a *pecking order*, learnt through a series of skirmishes. Junior birds always defer to seniors and a bird rarely changes its place in this hierarchy.

• TERRITORY •

A *territory* is a patch of ground that an animal defends against intruders to preserve some commodity in short supply, usually food. It is generally a permanent arrangement – a tawny owl defends its territory throughout its adult life. In contrast, a fieldfare defends a bush only as long as there are berries on it. Both the owl and fieldfare find it worthwhile to spend time and energy defending territories because an exclusive food supply gives them an easy living. A fieldfare defends windfalls against other thrushes but if flocks of ravenous birds invade, defence is futile. Likewise, a glut of berries in the neighbourhood means there is no point defending a personal supply.

Another commodity is breeding space. The male defends the territory, sometimes with the help of the female. Pairs of tits, thrushes and wrens need an assured food supply for their families but some birds, especially hole-nesters, only defend the immediate vicinity of their nests.

Standing guard *A fieldfare* (right) *attacks a blackbird to prevent it stealing an apple.*

Nest-hole territory *A starling* (below) *only defends the tree where it is nesting.*

As well as providing a haven for rearing the family, the spacing effect of territories reduces predation. If a magpie steals eggs from one nest, it will search nearby for more. Its chance of finding any is small if nests are spaced apart.

Where birds defend food, territory size depends on its abundance. In times of plenty, each bird can survive in a smaller space, so more birds squeeze in. Birds without territories do not breed and may even starve. They constantly watch for a space and the death of a territory-holder will result in its rapid replacement.

TERRITORIES OF SOME COMMON BIRDS

Blackbird	All year	2000 m² (2400 yd²)	These figures are app-
Chaffinch	Breeding	7000 m² (8400 yd²)	roximate: territory size
Goldfinch	Breeding	240 m² (290 yd²)	is elastic and individual
Great spotted woodpecker	All year	5+ ha (12+ acres)	territories vary accord-
Great tit	Breeding	1.2 ha (3 acres)	ing to the suitability of
Marsh tit	All year	3 ha (7 acres)	the habitat. In general,
Robin	All year	1–1.5 ha (2¹/₂–3¹/₂ acres)	the larger territories are
Song thrush	All year	2000 m² (2400 yd²)	used for feeding; the
Starling	Breeding	1 m² (1¹/₅ yd²)	smaller ones are based
Swift	Breeding	Nest	around the nest sites and
Tawny owl	All year	20+ ha (50+ acres)	tend to shrink after the
Woodpigeon	Breeding	4000 m² (4800 yd²)	eggs have been laid.

∙: DISPLAYS AND FIGHTS :∙

BIRDS OFTEN COMMUNICATE by means of *displays*. These are gestures that are used as signals just as you might shake your fist or beckon with your finger. Displays send a basic message that conveys information to other birds about the mood and intentions of the signaller and are often used both in courtship and disputes. If a bird's aggressive displays are not successful in deterring rivals from taking food or territory, then full-blown fights may break out.

∙ INTENTION MOVEMENTS ∙

The simplest form of communication is the small movements a bird makes as it prepares to do something, such as crouching slightly before taking off. These *intention movements* – often too quick to see – co-ordinate the actions of flocks or convey more detailed information. The reaction of woodpigeons, for example, to one of the flock taking off depends on subtle changes in behaviour. If the bird shows the normal intention movements, it can fly away without disturbing the others. But if it takes off suddenly, the others take this as an alarm signal and the entire flock flies off.

Taking off
A woodpigeon in a hurry will alert its companions to danger.

∙ DISPLAYS ∙

Displays are signals used both in disputes, to settle arguments without coming to blows, and in courtship, to reduce the aggression between mates. Some are intention movements or other actions, such as preening, that have been exaggerated to signal a stronger message. During courtship the male mallard makes preening actions that show off his *speculum* (the colourful "badge" on the wings). You are most likely to see displays when birds confront each other at close quarters. The

Warning display *A greenfinch lifts its wings, as if intending to fly forward to attack.*

same displays are often used both in courting and quarrelling so, unless you can identify the sexes, you cannot always tell what is happening, especially as a male's initial reaction to a female arriving in his territory is often aggressive. When birds gather at a birdfeeder, squabbles break out because they encroach on normal individual distances (p.142). If every argument ended in a fight, birds would not only waste time better spent feeding but they might also get hurt. Instead, disputes are settled with displays that indicate motivation so a bird can judge how aggressive another is and either retreat or stand its ground.

• THREATS AND SUBMISSIONS •

In a threat display, a bird looks menacing by including elements of attack behaviour but stops short of coming to blows. The bird fluffs its feathers, points its bill at its rival or raises its wings as if about to fly at it. Submission is signalled by a display in which the bird asks not to be attacked by sleeking its feathers and crouching.

Display postures are often enhanced by the bird's plumage. If you watch great tits on the bird-table, you will see that male great tits display (by showing off their broad breast-stripes) more often than the females, which have narrower stripes.

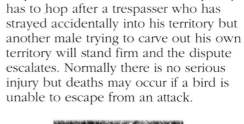

Show of strength *A male great tit shows off his broad breast-stripe and spreads his wings to force a blue tit away from a fat-filled log.*

• FIGHTS •

When fighting does break out, it is most common among strangers that have not learnt each other's social status, or between near-equals. An older, dominant bird easily displaces its junior but one of about the same rank will hold its ground. The two square up to each other and, as their displays become stronger, a fight may break out. A blackbird usually only has to hop after a trespasser who has strayed accidentally into his territory but another male trying to carve out his own territory will stand firm and the dispute escalates. Normally there is no serious injury but deaths may occur if a bird is unable to escape from an attack.

Blue tits fighting *One blue tit pins another by its legs in a dispute over seeds. Fights may look nasty but they are usually over in a few seconds and there is rarely any injury.*

Blue tit

Escalated dispute *Two garden tits exchange blows on a peanut bag.*

Coal tit

∴ SONGS AND CALLS ∵

A S WELL AS DISPLAYS, voice is an important means of communication for birds. Songs vary in their complexity between species and are a useful way of identifying birds. A subsong, a quieter version of the full song that can be heard outside the main song period, is largely the sound of young males. Many birds also have a vocabulary of simple calls, used especially when they are living together in flocks or mated pairs, but the exact meaning of each is not known for every species.

· WHAT ARE BIRDS SAYING? ·

It is a shame that songs which give us so much pleasure are used by birds principally as a means of threatening each other. (The consolation is that songs are a means of avoiding outright fighting.) Singing is most intense during the season when birds are taking up their territories. A bird will sing most vehemently when a stranger intrudes; once they have settled down, neighbours take little notice of each other.

Songster *The dunnock sometimes sings while flying in search of its mate.*

However, song is also used by males to advertise for a mate. Ornithologists have found evidence that suggests that the females of some species, like the robin and dunnock, choose their mates on the qualities of their songs, such as the time they spend singing or the rate at which they sing. It may be that the best songsters are the healthiest males or those with territories containing a plentiful supply of food, so they promise to be the best providers for a family. A rich and varied song may be the sound equivalent of elaborate plumage, like the peacock's train, which is designed to dazzle the female into accepting a mate. A bachelor robin sings more than a robin with a mate and some birds stop singing completely when they have formed a pair. Others continue singing as a means of strengthening the pair bond and maintaining the female in breeding condition.

Some people have the enviable gift of being able to remember and instantly recognize the songs and calls of birds. The rest of us have to spend some time each spring seeking out singing birds, identifying them and familiarizing ourselves again with the songs that we had forgotten over the winter. Even then, there are usually a few species' songs that we find difficult,

especially when a bird has a varied repertoire or its song can be confused with another's. It helps jog our memory if we can put words to the songs, as with the *"Little bit of bread and no cheese"* sound of the yellowhammer (a member of the bunting family), or the chaffinch's *"Sweet, will you-will you, kiss-me-dear?"*. (The descriptions of songs and calls in *Bird Profiles* are designed as a similar memory aid.)

Marking territory *A reed bunting sings out loud from its regular song-post.*

· SIMPLE AND VARIED SONGS ·

One long-standing puzzle is why some birds have simple songs and are content to repeat *cuckoo* (or a similarly monotonous phrase) maybe hundreds of times, while others have the most varied outpourings of warbles and trills. An individual robin, for example, has a repertoire of several hundred phrases, with about four used in each song-cycle. The sequence is constantly changing so each robin's song is never the same twice. The value of this complexity seems to be that the singer persuades other males to settle elsewhere by fooling them into thinking that a patch of ground is packed with rivals. If a male robin has such a varied number of notes

and a female robin perceives them as coming from a possible mate, how does the male manage to sing the right notes and how does the female recognize them? The answer is that a bird's song is partly inherited from its parents (or instinctive) but also learnt from other birds that it hears, sometimes while still in the nest. It grows up listening to the males of its species singing in neighbouring gardens and uses the memory of their notes to compose its own song.

A young chaffinch starts to sing when it leaves the nest, but its first song is a quiet, rambling medley of chirps and rattles, known as the *subsong*. This seems to be a

Robin's complex song *We, and other robins, can recognize the song of a robin (right), despite the huge number of possible notes because there is an overall similarity in the pattern of the phrases that distinguishes the song from, say, that of a goldcrest (above).*

147

form of practice. The chaffinch stops singing during the winter and starts again in spring when it establishes its first territory. The subsong now changes, becoming louder and closer to the adult's, but without the three clearly defined phrases (p.147) that are characteristic of the full song. Eventually the young bird confidently sings the full song, although it will practise with subsongs each spring.

Many garden birds sing for most of the year, except when busy chick-rearing or moulting. An autumn burst of song will coincide with the time that some birds establish a territory and often find a mate. Cold weather disrupts these activities, but you can still hear some song on fine winter days. Then, in spring, the air becomes filled with song from dawn to dusk as the birds finally settle down to breed.

· DAWN CHORUS ·

Morning sound *A song thrush leads the dawn chorus.*

Tree-top perch

At no time is the chorus of song so intense as at dawn, when the first notes ring out in a dark world. As it becomes light there is a crescendo of sound, with different species joining in, and the full dawn chorus continues for about half an hour. Why birds should choose to sing so vehemently at dawn has long been a mystery. It would seem that, after the long night's fast, their priority should be eating a large breakfast.

Several answers have been suggested. One is that, contrary to expectation, a full stomach is not a good idea for small birds because the increased weight makes flying more strenuous. Therefore the birds delay feeding and fill in the time with singing. Another idea is that it is difficult to find food in the dark and insect prey is sluggish (and thus difficult to spot) in the early morning chill. In both cases, it may also be useful right at the start of the day to remind neighbours not to trespass. But as with birdsong itself, there is probably no single explanation of the dawn chorus.

Early bird *Small birds, such as the* wren *(left),* may prefer to spend the early hours singing rather than feeding.

Dawn silhouette *A male blackbird* (right) *sings as dawn breaks. The dawn chorus starts sooner after moonlit nights.*

·CALL NOTES·

As well as their songs, birds make use of a number of calls that cover a variety of meanings. The great tit, for example, has over a dozen different calls for particular contexts. Calls are used to co-ordinate the behaviour of birds by telling one another of their intentions or feelings.

The simplest communication is to broadcast one's position to other birds with *contact notes*. Shrill notes accompany a small flock of tits as they make their way along a hedge or fly between trees. These notes keep the members of the flock together while they are searching for insects, often out of each other's sight.

When a cat tries to sneak up on the bird-table, its attempt to get within striking distance is frustrated by *alarm calls* (simple, harsh *chat* notes) from a vigilant bird. Birds of all species recognize this sound and, as soon as the call is uttered, fly up to the safety of trees.

The call is also used for mobbing owls. When an owl is discovered on its daytime perch, birds gather around to scold it. Their cries alert other birds which are drawn to the scene and the owl often has to abandon its perch for a quieter site. By drawing attention to a cat or an owl the

Contact call *A female mallard quacks loudly to her mate.*

Broad bill

birds destroy its chances of making a catch. A different tactic is pursued against birds of prey. When a hawk is spotted, the birds withdraw into foliage and utter thin *see* calls that warn other birds of the danger overhead. Unlike calls made in response to the cat or owl, the hawk alarm is ventriloquial and hard to pinpoint so the birds sounding the call do not give away their positions.

Territorial call *A male rook caws and spreads his tail to declare ownership of a nest site.*

∴ PAIR-FORMATION ∵

PAIR-FORMATION IS INTIMATELY connected with territorial behaviour. The songs and displays described on previous pages, which are used for defending the territory, often have the dual purpose of attracting mates. Courtship allows birds to choose the best partner. Males, while jealously fending off rivals, help their mates prepare for nesting. While the females undertake the manufacture of the eggs and most of the nesting work, the males of some species help feed their mates.

• COURTSHIP •

As well as giving a bird the chance to choose a suitable mate, courtship reduces the natural animosity between two individuals that normally results in their keeping their distance (p.142). The male's first instinct is to drive intruders away from his territory but, by holding her ground and acting submissively, a female establishes her presence and the male starts to court her. Pair-formation may then be so quick as to be almost instantaneous but some birds take a week or so before becoming fully paired, especially if they are courting for the first time.

The female bird does not necessarily choose to stay with the first male who courts her. The pairings that took place in autumn are not always confirmed in spring because both members of a pair may not be fortunate enough to survive a harsh winter. However, if members of a couple do not die, they are likely to pair up again. Familiarity and experience help courtship to proceed rapidly and nesting to start early in the year. This is an advantage because, with tits at least, the earliest clutches of eggs produce the most young.

Current research demonstrates that female birds are somehow able to determine which males will make good "husbands and fathers". These are likely to be the older and more experienced birds. The key to survival is the ability to find food efficiently. A mature male is living proof that he has successfully learnt to survive through hard times and so will be more likely to find enough food to sustain a growing family in the future. The female bird, therefore,

Two for joy *A pair of magpies perch together.*

Mallard "rape"
Sometimes mallard drakes, such as this albino, forgo preliminary courtship routines and take females by force.

has to be able to recognize an old male. He will have a more elaborate song (p.147) or, as with chaffinches, be more ardent in his advances towards her. Young males do not display as vigorously or pursue unwilling females, whereas an older male will fervently chase a female across neighbouring territories in order to entice her to come back.

Bowing display *The male dove bows and circles before his chosen female with his neck-feathers puffed out and tail fanned.*

• MATE GUARDING •

The pair are often inseparable before egg-laying. Roosting and feeding together is not a sign of devotion, as early naturalists fondly believed. If a human emotion can be given, then it is jealousy. You can see this in street pigeons: a male *drives* his mate, walking so closely behind her that he almost trips over her tail. If she takes off, he will follow her and the pair fly

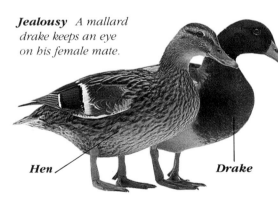

Jealousy *A mallard drake keeps an eye on his female mate.*

Hen

Drake

wing-tip to wing-tip, banking and gliding in unison. The male guards his mate to ensure that he alone will be the father of her eggs. On the other hand, he will take advantage of any lapses in his neighbour's vigilance to cuckold him. There is a clear benefit for the male if he can father extra offspring, but there may also be an advantage to the female. For instance, if a male dunnock mates with a female, he will help rear her offspring, so by "taking lovers" a female dunnock recruits extra providers for her family (p.10). A male starling sometimes takes another mate but, as he only feeds the first set of nestlings, the second family is often unsuccessful. The male wren regularly builds more than one nest but usually only mates with one female. Sometimes, he will entice a second into a spare nest if he occupies a territory containing enough food to rear two families.

• COURTSHIP FEEDING •

As the female prepares for nesting, the male often presents her with food. Female tits, for instance, require 40% extra food to form their eggs. Courtship feeding continues while the female is incubating and reduces the time that she has to spend off the nest. Some ornithologists believe that courtship feeding may help to strengthen the bond between a pair, especially where, as in some species, the males only go through the motions of presenting food. It also seems that some females use the male's ability to supply food during courtship as an indication of how good he will be at providing for the future family.

"Kissing" coots *Although courtship feeding usually ceases when the male starts feeding the young, the male coot may continue to offer tit-bits even after the chicks have hatched.*

•: NEST-BUILDING :•

THE NEST IS A CONTAINER for eggs (and later nestlings) that keeps them warm and protects them from enemies. Although not a hard-and-fast rule, birds whose young leave the nest shortly after hatching, such as mallards and pheasants, build simple nests – often no more than a scrape in the ground – while those whose young remain in the nest until they can fly build elaborate nests. Most of the common garden birds build cup-shaped nests but several kinds prefer to nest in holes.

•SELECTING A SITE•

At various times in late winter and spring, you can see birds hopping from twig to twig along a hedge or around the boughs of a tree. Although not looking for food, they are clearly searching for something. Their particular interest in forks of branches shows that they are prospecting for nest sites. For many garden birds choosing the site, and building the nest, is the responsibility of the female, although she may be helped by the male. (The male wren is unusual in that he builds the

Half-built nest *A pair of rooks add sticks to their untidy nest, underpinned by a fork between branches. They may steal twigs from neighbouring nests in the rookery.*

nest alone.) For hole-nesting tits, starlings, pied flycatchers and redstarts, however, it is the male who chooses the nest site.

How a nest site is selected remains something of a mystery. We can imagine that the bird is looking for a suitable configuration of twigs or some other foundation that will give a solid base to the nest. Protection from predators and shelter from the elements are other considerations,

Mud   *Leaves and needles*

Feathers   *Moss*

Paper and tissue   *Dry grasses*

Common material *A variety of nest material is chosen for its structural support and insulation. Availability is a key factor: birds tend to use what is easy to collect.*

although birds often nest in unsatisfactorily exposed places. This may be either because the builder is inexperienced or because there is a shortage of suitable sites. In gardens where undergrowth and tangled foliage are discouraged, good sites are scarce and birds have to make do with second-best nesting-places. Occasionally a bird becomes confused and wastes time building a series of nests. This happens where the bird is faced with a multiple-choice situation that does not occur in nature, such as that posed by the rungs of a ladder or a pile of drainpipes.

· STARTING THE NEST ·

It is amazing to think that the long-tailed tit's fragile ball of lichens, cobwebs and feathers, the magpie's lattice dome of sticks and the thrush's cup-nest of woven grasses and twigs are built with only the bill (sometimes assisted by the feet) as a tool. The most difficult part of the construction is the foundation, and jackdaws may drop barrowloads of twigs down a chimney before one wedges satisfactorily to allow building to proceed. When a chaffinch starts its nest, it makes secure anchor points by wrapping strands of spiders' web around twigs. Moss and grass are then added to make a firm cushion. The bird sits on this pad, works more material into place by pulling at it with its bill. It forms the cup shape by pushing with its breast and scrabbling with its feet until the materials become felted together (p.154).

Building with the bill *A long-tailed tit places another piece of lichen to the lip of its nearly completed, dome-shaped nest.*

As a rule, nest-building takes longer at the start of the season because work will stop temporarily in cold weather. Once complete, the nest may remain empty for several days before egg-laying starts.

It is surprising that so many nests, which are such a struggle to make, are abandoned after only one brood and that birds do not re-use them to save the effort of building another. Although rooks and house martins regularly refurbish their old nests in spring, and blackbirds sometimes re-use an old nest, many nests are beyond repair after a winter's wind and rain. Tits and swallows rear their second brood of the year in a brand-new nest, probably to cut down on infestation by fleas and other parasites or, in the case of the tits, because their old nests were squashed flat by the first set of nestlings.

After the storm *A moorhen patches up its nest with reeds. After eggs have been laid, the nest may need repairing due to flood damage.*

· NEST TYPES ·

Building the nest takes great time and energy. A pair of woodpeckers may take a month or more, working several hours a day, to chisel out their hole. Thrushes take up to three weeks to make their solid cups, while finches finish their delicate constructions in a week or so. Tits may face a huge job if they have to pad out all the space in a large cavity or nest-box.

With practice it is possible to identify nests after their occupants have abandoned them. Pay particular attention to the shape of the nest, the materials that have been used and the general pattern of construction. Do not be surprised to find string, metal foil or paper in the structure of the nest. Some birds will incorporate all sorts of litter.

Blue tit The blue tit's nest *(above)*, made from moss mixed with pine twigs and grass, has adopted the oblong shape of the nest-box it was built in.

Spotted flycatcher A shaded place with a good view is a favoured site for this rather untidy, loose nest *(top right)* of woven moss, roots and grass. It is lined with feathers, hair and dead leaves. The exterior is often decorated with cobwebs.

Greenfinch The deep cup *(above)* of twigs, grass and moss, lined with fine roots, is usually built high up in a thick shrub, often an evergreen.

Chaffinch The nest *(left)* is made of grass and moss, lined with roots and feathers. It is decorated outside with lichen.

Swallow The swallow's shallow saucer-shaped nest *(right)*, lined with feathers, is composed of mud, usually mixed with grasses and other plant fibre. The nest is often situated on a ledge in sheds, garages or other open buildings.

Goldcrest Suspended, like a hammock, from a conifer branch, the deep cup-shaped nest *(below)* is made from moss and spiders' webs and lined with feathers.

Dunnock The neat cup-nest *(above)* of plant roots, grass, leaves and moss is built, usually in a thick hedge, on a foundation of twigs. The nest is lined with wool and hair, or sometimes feathers.

Wren The nest *(above)*, often found in a cavity in a wall, is a feather-lined, hollow ball constructed from moss and grass.

Long-tailed tit The feather-lined mass of moss *(right)* is bound by cobwebs to twigs and covered with lichen.

∴ EGGS AND INCUBATION ∴

THE SHAPE, COLOUR AND texture of birds' eggs have long
been admired but the development of the bird inside and
the behaviour of the parents in nurturing their eggs are just as
worthy of our interest. Egg production is such a strain on the
female that it is not surprising that there is often a gap between
the building of the nest and the start of egg-laying while she
concentrates on feeding, or that the females of so many species
need their mates to supply them with extra food.

· THE NUMBER OF EGGS ·

Formation of the egg inside the female's
body starts several days before laying.
The fertilized egg, consisting mainly of
yolk, moves down the oviduct where it
is coated in albumen (the egg white) and
where the shell is added. Production of
the eggs is a time of strain for the female
and saps her of energy and body reserves.
The shell, for instance, which takes about
a day to make, requires so much calcium
that the bird has to borrow it from her
bones. The females of some species
become less active before laying and
roost at night in the nest so that they use
less energy to keep warm.

Most garden birds lay their eggs in the
morning at 24-hour intervals, but pigeons,
herons, owls and swifts lay at longer

Coal tit egg *The normal clutch
of 7–12 eggs may weigh as
much as the coal tit itself.*

intervals. If the clutch is lost, through
predation or the nest being blown down,
most birds lay a replacement clutch.

Some birds, such as pigeons and gulls,
lay a fixed number of eggs in each clutch
but for most garden birds the clutch size
depends on the amount of food the
females can gather. The figures given
in *Bird Profiles* state the average range
of egg numbers. In bad weather, the swift
lays two, rather than three, eggs and
house martins lay smaller, "runt" eggs.
The tawny owl and kestrel may not even

*Blackbird
egg*

Nightingale egg

Clutch size (above) *The nightingale usually
lays one clutch, unlike the blackbird, which
may lay up to five clutches in one season.*

Cup-nest *A bullfinch's neat cup-nest* (left)
shows its average clutch of five eggs.

attempt to lay if there is a shortage of mice and voles. The smaller clutches laid by some garden birds indicate that gardens are not such a good habitat as woods. There is a variation with geography and climate, so that birds in northern countries lay more eggs than those in the south. Scandinavian robins lay, on average, one more egg than Spanish robins. German tits are more likely to lay a second clutch than British ones.

The number of broods also depends on food supply. The crop of caterpillars is short-lived (because they pupate) so tits, which feed on them, usually manage only a single brood; blackbirds with their wide diet can rear several broods. If frost or drought makes the ground too hard to dig for worms, blackbirds start nesting late or stop early, laying fewer clutches. Bullfinches and goldfinches continue into September in years when their favourite plants are seeding well.

Chaffinch nest *A clutch of four eggs is kept warm by the insulating quality of the characteristic hair, wool and feather lining. The chaffinch stops nesting by midsummer, when the rich crop of insects, which provides food for its growing young, is over.*

· THE COLOUR OF EGGS ·

White is the basic colour of birds' eggs but most species add pigments to them as an aid to camouflage. The shell is coated with pigment as it passes down the oviduct. The background colour is added first, before the layers of the shell are built up, and the pattern is applied to the surface of the completed shell. If the egg is stationary as the pigment is applied, it appears as spots and splodges, and, if it is moving, streaks and lines are formed. Some hole-nesting birds, such as woodpeckers, tawny owls and little owls lay

Coloured eggs

Kestrel egg   *Crow egg*

White eggs

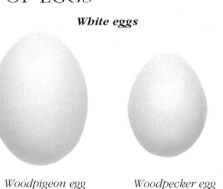

Woodpigeon egg   *Woodpecker egg*

glossy, white eggs – probably to make them show up in the dim recesses so that the parents do not trample on them. In the relative security of a hole, there is no need for the eggs to be camouflaged. Woodpigeons, which also have white eggs, have little need for camouflage because they start incubating once the first egg is laid. Birds that lay their eggs in open nests, such as kestrels, crows, thrushes and finches, have speckled and coloured eggs that blend in with the surrounding wood and foliage.

• INCUBATION •

Birds are warm-blooded and the chicks inside the eggs need to be kept warm by the adult birds sitting on them in the nest. Shortly before the eggs are laid, feathers are shed from the adult's breast to form a bare patch of skin. (Ducks pluck their breast-feathers for a nest lining.) The rich supply of blood vessels to this *brood*

patch makes it act as a hotpad for transferring body heat efficiently to the eggs. If you can feel a brood patch when holding a bird, it is a sure sign that the bird is incubating, except for pigeons and doves, which have a bare patch all year.

Incubation does not usually start until the clutch is complete: although the parent bird sits on the nest before this time, it does not use its brood patch.

When incubating properly, the adult ruffles its feathers to expose the brood patch before settling down and tucking the eggs into place. Once on the eggs, the bird is rather restless, but it will freeze still if it senses danger. At intervals, it stands up and pokes the eggs with its bill to shuffle them around. This has several

Duty *A female bullfinch* (left) *incubates eggs.*

Egg roll *By rotating the eggs, a street pigeon* (below) *makes sure they are evenly warmed.*

functions: it allows air to circulate so the embryos inside the eggs can breathe (by air diffusing through the shell) and rearranges the eggs so they are evenly warmed. Turning the eggs is also necessary for the embryos to develop properly.

With the majority of garden birds, incubation is carried out by the female alone. Where the male shares incubation, he also develops a brood patch. This is the case with the starling, although the female is on the nest throughout the night and for most of the day. Male woodpeckers do most of the incubation, however, and sit at night. Swifts swap places every two hours or so. The sitting bird does not remain on the nest continuously during each shift, but takes a number of breaks to feed, defecate or indulge in a bout of preening. Even when the male brings her food, the female will leave the nest. You

Egg-warmer *A blue tit gauges the temperature of its eggs to within a few degrees.*

can see female tits pop out of nest-boxes and flutter their wings excitedly as they receive beakfuls of caterpillars.

Incubation is more than just sitting on the clutch. The sitting bird has to monitor the temperature of the eggs (which it probably does while shuffling them) and regulate it accordingly. The amount of heat needed to keep the eggs warm depends on the nest insulation and the weather. Sunny days allow incubating birds to stay off the nest for longer than wet, windy weather. Although developing chicks are surprisingly resistant to becoming chilled, too much exposure will slow down development, perhaps fatally.

• HATCHING •

Because incubation usually starts only when the clutch is complete, all the eggs in a clutch hatch together. Owls and pigeons are exceptions – incubation starts immediately with the first egg and the owlets and squabs hatch out in sequence.

Hatching is a difficult part of a bird's life. It starts a few days before the nestling eventually emerges, with the young bird shifting its position in the egg and pushing its bill into the air sac in the blunt end of the shell to begin breathing. It then

Ring of holes *A series of holes* (above) *is punched around the blunt end of the shell by a moorhen chick. Strong muscles in the back of its neck power the egg-tooth, enabling the hatching chick to break out.*

Pushing free *A magpie chick* (left) *shoves the shell apart by pushing with its feet and heaving with its neck and shoulders – it now wears the blunt end like a cap.*

hammers a hole in the shell using its bill, protected by a horny, white *egg-tooth*, which can still be seen on nestlings that are a day or two old. This activity is called *pipping* and is the first visible sign that the egg is about to hatch.

Several hours elapse before the final phase, which takes less than an hour. The chick punches a ring of holes in the shell to weaken it before forcing the cap off. Once its head is free, it rapidly struggles out of the broken shell and lies, curled up and exhausted, in the bottom of the nest.

In the wide world *A blind, newly hatched blackbird rests curled up after struggling free of the eggshell that has protected the bird until now. The white egg-tooth is still visible.*

∴ CHICK-REARING ∴

YOUNG BIRDS OF THE most common species – song-birds, pigeons, woodpeckers and birds of prey – hatch in an almost helpless state and stay in the nest until they are ready to fly. They are usually called *nestlings*. In contrast, young gulls, coots and moorhens (known as *chicks*) leave the nest quickly but are fed by their parents, while a few, such as mallard and pheasant, even feed themselves, under their mothers' protection.

• FEEDING THE YOUNG •

When young birds hatch out they are weak and wet with egg fluids. Their parents brood them to keep them warm. As they grow stronger, they are left alone while both adults collect food, but brooding resumes at night and in bad weather until the nestlings are well grown.

Feeding the family keeps the parents busy all day. Males that played no part in nest-building or incubation help rear their families by bringing food. Most young birds are fed on insects and other invertebrates, such as spiders, snails and worms. Even the vegetarian finches give their young some animal food, because it contains more of the protein, calcium and other nutrients needed by growing bodies. It also holds more fluids so the young birds do not need to drink. Collecting insects can be hard work, especially in bad weather. It takes 10,000 caterpillars and a hundred times as many aphids to raise a family of blue tits, so it is not surprising that nesting birds lose weight.

When a parent bird returns with food, the nestlings automatically open their mouths in a wide gape. Before their eyes have opened, they gape when they feel the vibration of the parent landing at the nest. Later, they respond to the sight of its arrival and direct their gape towards it.

Two types of young *Like the young of many other ground-nesting birds, a moorhen chick leaves the nest soon after hatching* (above). *With open eyes, large feet and a downy coat, it is better developed than its tree-nesting counterparts. A young nightingale, for example, is 11 or 12 days old before it leaves the nest* (right).

The brightly coloured inside of the mouth acts as a signal for the parent to push food into it. The parent bird feeds the nearest nestling without any attempt to share the food fairly. This results in the strongest nestling getting the most food, but when it is full it will stop begging and the others get a share. In this way all the nestlings' hunger is satisfied – providing that there is enough food to go around. If not, some nestlings may starve. However, more young birds will grow up in the long run if the parents can rear a few well-fed individuals rather than many half-starved ones.

Gaping Three-day-old blue tit nestlings, still naked and blind, beg for food by craning their necks and pointing their bright yellow mouths upwards.

· CLEANING THE NEST ·

If you have birds nesting in your garden, look for empty eggshells on the lawn. Once the eggs have hatched, the parent bird removes the broken shells. Another chore is to remove the nestlings' droppings. When a nestling has been fed, it turns and presents its posterior to the parent, who either swallows the droppings or removes them from the nest.

If droppings were left, the nest would become messy, with the dangers of clogging the nestlings' new feathers and maybe spreading disease. It is also important to remove the white stains around the nest because they might attract predators. This is not a concern for birds, like swallows and martins, that nest in safe places; their droppings foul walls and paths.

Eggshell

Birch tree

Clearing up One of the first tasks of a parent starling is to remove the eggshells of hatched nestlings from its nest hole. They are a danger because they could trap or cut a young bird.

When the nestlings are ready to fly, they deposit droppings on the rim of the nest, so an empty but soiled nest is evidence that the family was raised successfully. (Unhatched eggs and dead nestlings are usually removed or buried in the nest material, so an empty nest does not necessarily equal successful parenthood.)

Soiled nest *As their nest is safely tucked away from predators among garage rafters, swallows* (above) *do not need to clear away droppings.*

Toilet toil *After feeding its nestlings, a blue tit* (right) *removes a faecal sac.*

• FLEDGING •

By the time the young birds have their feathers, they have grown to the point where they are almost bursting out of the nest. Resist the temptation to visit them because they will try to escape by leaping out of the nest even though they cannot fly properly. This is a defence against predators which, although dangerous, is better than staying in the nest and being eaten. Even without disturbance, young birds leave the nest before their feathers are fully grown. You can recognize these *fledglings*, as they are now called, because their tails and wings look stumpy and

they do not yet have the effortless grace of their elders. It is worth leaving the nest as soon as they can fly to reduce the threat of predation: birds that grow up in open cup-nests fly at an earlier age than those that are brought up in the greater safety of nests sited in holes. (Compare, for instance, the fledging times of cup-nesting finches with those of the hole-nesting tits in *Bird Profiles*.)

The fledging times in each species vary by a few days because the nestlings' growth depends on the abundance of food and the number of mouths in the nest that the parents have to feed. Swifts have an unusually variable fledging time because, in bad weather when flying insects are scarce, their nestlings conserve their energy and virtually stop growing.

For the first few days after leaving the nest, most fledglings do not fly much and rest quietly in a secluded spot, such as a dense hedge, where they wait patiently for their parents to bring them food. As

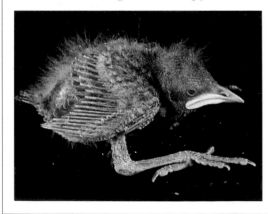

Unfledged starling *A starling, at about 10 days old, has tubular feather sheaths, from which the tips of its wing-feathers emerge.*

their feathers grow and they become more confident, they can follow their parents and save them the effort of flying to and fro with every beakful of food. Watch for young starlings following on their parents' heels as they forage on the lawn. The adults have only to turn to push the food into a waiting mouth. Males of some species take charge of feeding just before the young become independent if the females start another clutch.

Call for assistance *A blue tit fledgling contacts its parents after it has flown the nest.*

· LAUNCH INTO INDEPENDENCE ·

Stories that birds teach their young to fly are incorrect. The ability to fly is instinctive and a tit in a cramped nest-box or a house martin under the eaves hardly has a chance to open its wings before it launches itself into the air. It is amazing how capable the young bird is on its first flight. The complex wing movements that drive a bird through the air and the delicate balance (much more intricate than that needed for riding a bicycle!) are present and correct from the start. It will take practice, however, to perfect the art of maneouvring and landing.

Parents sometimes encourage young birds that seem unwilling to fly. Young swifts leave the nest on their own and

become independent immediately but house martin parents, together with other adults, entice their brood out of the nest (often under the eaves of a house) by calling to them as they slowly fly past (p.52). They accompany them on their first flight and, if a young martin crash-lands, the adults will circle around it and encourage it to fly back to the nest.

Early learners *Pheasant chicks* (above) *have a longer incubation period than common garden birds and are equipped to leave the nest a few hours after hatching. They fly after about two weeks.*

Maiden flight *A juvenile swift* (left) *takes to the air with amazing confidence on its first flight from its nest under the eaves of a house. Once it has started to fly, the swift may not land again for a long time.*

∵ MOVEMENTS ∵

THROUGHOUT THEIR LIVES, birds are continually on the move. The distance they move over may be no more than that travelled daily from roosts to feeding-grounds. Movements may be made seasonally within a country, such as from woodland in summer to gardens in winter, or at random, as food runs out in a particular area. Some species of bird migrate over tremendous distances, between continents.

· MIGRATION ·

Every spring in Europe we eagerly wait for migrants to return from their winter in warmer countries. We watch for martins, swallows and swifts darting overhead, for warblers and flycatchers flitting among the newly opening foliage and listen out for the first cuckoo. Then, at the end of summer, these birds slip away again and we watch, with less pleasure, for the heralds of winter, the redwings and fieldfares escaping harsher northern winters. The notion that these birds are migrants while those that stay with us are residents is a simplification of the swirling pattern of bird movements. *Migration* can be defined as any journey that involves a bird changing its home – that is, the area where it carries out its everyday activities of feeding and roosting.

By this definition, a great tit is migrating when it leaves its summer home in the woods and settles in a suburban garden for the winter. This change in lifestyle fulfils the main function of migration, allowing the tit to exploit two habitats and sources of food – the crop of caterpillars in the woods and the peanuts in the garden. To distinguish between movements that range from the few miles of the great tit to the thousands covered by the swift or the swallow returning from South Africa, it is convenient to speak of the latter as *true migration*.

True migration is not rigid. Every year, some swallows and house martins linger long after most migrant birds have left. A few, seen as late in the year as early December, are genuine late departures

True migrant
The swift is able to cover 500 miles in a day when it undertakes its winter journey to Africa.

that have managed to find enough insects to sustain them until they finally decide to go. Others, seen in February, could be early arrivals, but the third group, seen around Christmas and New Year, usually consists of birds that have lost the urge to migrate. Although swallows and martins are unlikely to find enough flying insects to survive the winter, some warblers have begun to overwinter in Britain, and a few hundred chiffchaffs find enough insects each year to forgo the flight south.

· PARTIAL MIGRANTS ·

When Carolus Linnaeus, the eighteenth-century naturalist, gave animals and plants their scientific names (p.188), he called the chaffinch *Fringilla coelebs* – Latin for bachelor finch. He had noticed that the few chaffinches that remained for the winter in his native Sweden were nearly all males. Most of the females, as well as a few males, had migrated south. In Britain, Germany and the Netherlands, male chaffinches are also in the majority during winter, while countries with milder climates receive an influx of the females that have left the northern countries.

Movement of part of a population (which may also be a certain age group) is called a *partial migration*. Unless you keep detailed records of

Bachelor finch *The male chaffinch is left behind in winter.*

Immigrant jackdaw *The jackdaw is a partial migrant; the number of jackdaws in Great Britain increases in winter because of an influx of birds arriving from colder European countries. Other frequent immigrants to British shores include numbers of starlings, blackbirds, blue tits and chaffinches.*

numbers, you are unlikely to notice partial migration. Because of its mild winters, Britain receives thousands of birds from countries with a more severe, continental climate. The discerning eye can sometimes identify the visitors. Seen close-up, continental blue tits appear larger and brighter than British birds. Visiting blackbirds and chaffinches feed in loose flocks while native birds lead more solitary lives around their summer homes.

Local movements is a term used for bird migration caused by a temporary food shortage. This may happen when a crop of berries has been consumed or when frost or snow makes animals and fallen seeds unobtainable. The two most obvious movements are the disappearance of ducks from frozen lakes, and the sudden arrival of redwings and fieldfares.

· IRRUPTIONS ·

In some winters there is a sudden invasion of birds, known as an *irruption*. This dramatic event occurs when a food supply fails in the birds' summer homes. The large numbers of birds that have built up in times of plenty are forced to move or perish. This chiefly happens to fruit- and seed-eating birds when plants produce poor crops, and to owls and hawks when rodent prey becomes scarce.

Conifers in northern Europe produce ample crops of seeds every two to four years, depending on the local climate but, in the years between, there may be an almost total failure to set seed. As a result, crossbills face starvation and come flooding south in search of food. Waxwings are another irrupting species and appear when rowan berries fail in northern forests. Tits, too, have been known to irrupt in their hundreds.

Irrupting species Sudden invasions of thousands of birds may occur when their chief food source is scarce. The great spotted woodpecker (above) *will arrive in large numbers when conifer seeds are in short supply. The jay* (right) *relies on acorns. In 1983, when acorns failed in Europe, large flocks of jays were seen coming into gardens to feed at peanut bags.*

· TRANSIENTS ·

One consequence of migration is that you will often see birds while they are on the way to a distant destination. They may stay for a few days to feed or to wait for a fair wind. These birds are known as *transients* or *birds of passage*. Many are common birds but the migration seasons of spring and autumn are exciting times because they also offer the chance to spot rare birds. Anything may turn up: from America, central Asia or the Arctic. Since migrating birds are sometimes caught up in storms and swept far off-course, they may appear thousands of miles from their normal route. These rare, disorientated visitors are called *accidentals*. Every autumn sees a few American birds turning up in western Europe. They set out to fly from North America, down the eastern seaboard to the tropics and beyond. Caught by westerly gales, they are carried across the Atlantic and deposited on European shores, with only a miraculous chance of returning.

· TIME TO GO ·

More than 250 years ago, naturalists realized that birds were not driven to migrate by hunger. Rather, they escape before food runs out: if they waited until starvation stared them in the face and were already losing condition, they would perish on the journey. Preparation for migration starts before departure time when birds fatten up with fuel for their journey. Once it is ready to fly, a bird's

In spring, there is less time for delay if the birds are to make the most of the summer plenty and rear as many offspring as possible. The migrants push north, hard on the heels of the retreating winter. Swallows spread northwards through Europe, approximately following the 8.9°C (48°F) isotherm, in a steady advance of about 25 miles per day, unless cold weather or a head-wind holds them up.

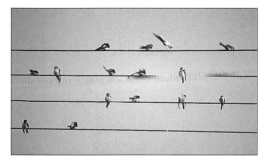

Pre-departure preparations *Before leaving, house martins* (above) *gather in flocks to perch on telephone wires, and the willow warbler* (right) *will switch its diet from insects to carbohydrate-rich berries.*

departure depends, to some extent, on the weather. It prefers to set off with favourable wind and weather.

Birds depart the country in a regular order. Those, like swifts, that rely on a healthy supply of insects depart early, while swallows and martins, which manage to scrape a living even when flying insects are scarce, stay longer. The change to a vegetarian diet also enables some warblers to dawdle. There is no urgency to leave and several weeks may elapse between the departure of the first individuals of a species and the final stragglers. Although birds are content to wait for the best weather for travelling, they are sometimes caught out: in September 1974, swallows became weatherbound on the wrong side of the Alps. Many died, but thousands were rescued in Switzerland, carried across the mountains and released in Italy.

Seasonal siskin *In autumn, the siskin flies from its nesting-place among conifers to birches, where it feeds on the seeds until it is time to migrate.*

∴ CURIOUS BEHAVIOUR ∴

THE PATTERNS OF BEHAVIOUR that have been detailed in the rest of this chapter are commonly in evidence around the garden. This is because they are widespread tactics that have evolved across each species to help the birds survive and raise a family successfully. However, from time to time, you may see birds engaged in some curious forms of behaviour, which may not seem to serve any particular purpose and which are frequently not at all easy to explain.

· STRETCHING AND YAWNING ·

Stretching and yawning are still not fully understood. They are called comfort movements, although their function is by no means as obvious as cleaning or scratching. After resting, especially if we have been sleeping or sitting in the same position for too long, we often stretch our arms and legs. From time to time, you can see birds in the garden do much the same thing: typically, they open out one wing for a second or two before folding it away again. Simultaneously, the leg on the same side of the body is extended and the tail is fanned. Some birds also stretch both wings together by raising them up over their backs.

An action that looks like stretching but with a different function may be seen if you are lucky enough to come across a kestrel or sparrowhawk eating its prey. The bird appears to be stretching both its wings in front of itself, but it is in fact crouching over its prey with its tail and wings spread. This activity is

Stretching *A collared dove* (above) *extends a leg and wing.*

Mantling *A young kestrel* (left) *shields its catch from other birds to make sure they do not steal it.*

called *mantling* and is used by the predator to hide its prey from other birds and prevent them from trying to steal it.

Why humans, birds and other animals stretch is not known for certain. The action may help to improve muscle tone or the blood circulation to the limbs. Yawning may be a form of stretching but it could also be a means of ensuring a full exchange of air in the lungs before a bird, or other animal, becomes fully active.

Full yawn *A black-headed gull gives a large yawn as it wakes up.*

· ANTING AND SMOKE-BATHING ·

Anting has been observed in many perching birds, especially jays but also starlings and blackbirds, yet its function is something of a mystery. The bird half-spreads its wings, twists its tail and wipes its bill on its flight-feathers, or else squats with its wings spread and tail pressed against the ground, as when sunbathing (p.136). A close look will reveal that the bird is on an ants' nest belonging to one of the ant species that squirts formic acid at enemies rather than stinging them. The bird either picks up the ants and rubs them against its feathers or, in the second version, passively lets them climb among its plumage. The best suggested explanation is that the formic acid helps kill parasitic feather lice.

Smoke-bathing is an odd form of anting, which is less common now that fewer people have homes with open fires.

Unusual antics *Twisting its tail, a jay spreads its wings to let ants run through its feathers.*

The bird, usually a crow, rook or starling, perches on a chimney-pot, or perhaps over a bonfire, and runs through the motions of anting, even placing "beakfuls" of smoke under its wings. (If you see birds simply perching on chimneys or other sources of smoke, they are more likely to be trying to keep warm.)

· ATTACKING WINDOWS ·

The sad fate of birds that accidentally crash into windows is discussed on page 182, but deliberately attacking windows is a different phenomenon. The usual explanation is that the bird has mistaken its reflection for a rival on its territory and is trying to drive it away. A carrion crow spent over an hour every day for a week attacking windows with its beak and claws so ferociously that the glass had to be cleaned of blood and saliva. The more common observation of birds tapping windows may be simply that the bird is baffled by the invisible barrier to its progress. There are stories of birds being given meals when the window is opened and then learning from the experience and tapping every day to request food.

· ACTS OF DESTRUCTION ·

Vandal *The great tit commits acts of wanton destruction.*

While we can accept that birds attack the blossom and fruit on our trees because they need to eat, it is hard to forgive apparently wanton destruction. Tits have long been known to come into houses and tear off loose wallpaper. This may be because they treat the paper as the flaking bark of a tree trunk and strip it to search for insects underneath. It is less easy to explain the tits' habit of pecking putty from window frames or the rubber seals on double-glazing units. As it has been noticed that they often attack putty after feeding at a nearby birdfeeder, it seems unlikely they are searching for hidden insect food. Birds and other animals sometimes go through the motions of hunting once they have eaten an easy meal (cats pounce on imaginary mice after they have been fed), so the tits may be following hunting habits after their easy meals of nuts.

Puzzling for two reasons is the house sparrows' habit of ripping apart primulas and crocuses. It is irritating to have a show of flowers ruined by sparrows tearing the petals or snipping off entire flowers. As they do not eat them, the only explanation for this bizarre activity seems to be sheer vandalism. It is also a mystery why they pick on yellow flowers in particular and hardly touch other colours.

Yellow primulas *These springtime flowers are often the victims of house sparrows, who tear them up and leave them on the ground.*

· CUCKOO HABITS ·

The cuckoo is an unusual visitor even to rural gardens, although you may hear one in nearby countryside. Occasionally, however, a cuckoo comes into a garden to look for nests in which to lay its eggs and leave them for the nests' owners to incubate. The nestling cuckoo later ejects the rightful occupants so it can receive the full attention of its hosts. The dunnock is a favourite victim but other, rarer hosts to this *brood parasite* range from blackbirds to wrens and goldcrests.

It is not so well known that other birds sometimes lay their eggs in host nests. The difference is that they choose nests

Trespasser *A starling egg lies broken on the garden path, having been ejected from the nest by the owner who realized it was not hers.*

of their own species. It has long been believed that the starlings' eggs frequently found on the ground near a nest had been laid by females "caught short". In fact, these are eggs that one female has laid in another's nest and that have been detected and removed by the nest-owner. However, once a starling has started to lay her own clutch she no longer discriminates against these interloping eggs and incubates them as her own.

Studies have shown that this "cuckoo" behaviour occurs in a number of other garden birds, such as swallows (especially when several pairs are nesting near each other). A swallow in the process of laying her eggs regularly has to leave the nest unattended while she feeds, and her neighbours take advantage of her absence to drop an egg into her nest.

Foster parent *A meadow pipit feeds a cuckoo out of the nest.*

Cuckoo egg

Robin eggs

Egg match A cuckoo removes a single egg from another bird's clutch and replaces it with one of its own. The egg, small for the size of a cuckoo, often mimics those of the host bird.

· FOSTER FEEDING ·

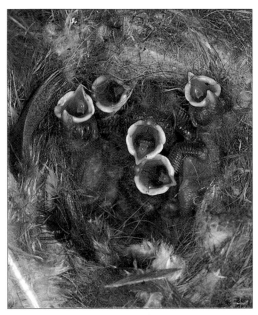

Home help *One family of blue tit nestlings in a tit-box benefited from the extra rations instinctively provided by a pair of wrens.*

It is instinctive for a parent bird to drop food into a brightly coloured opening. Normally this will be the mouth of one of its offspring but occasionally something goes wrong and the young of another bird benefits. Fledgling cuckoos collect meals from birds passing with food for their own youngsters but other birds also profit from mistakes in this instinctive behaviour. A song thrush that lost its own brood started to feed a young family of spotted flycatchers. These young birds had left the nest but were still begging for food, so they received an unusual supplementary diet of worms and caterpillars. We have to presume that the thrush's instinct to put food into gaping mouths was still "switched on", despite the loss of its family, so it easily swapped to feeding the flycatcher fledglings who were waiting for food from their parents. There is another story of a pair of wrens that not only fed a brood of blue tits in a nest-box but also removed their droppings.

CHAPTER FIVE

BIRD SURVIVAL

THERE ARE ENOUGH obstacles in the life of a garden bird to ensure that it will be lucky to live beyond a couple of years. The unfortunate majority die before they are a year old. Nothing you can do will alter these cruel facts or remove the many natural and man-made dangers. All the same, it is hard to ignore an individual bird that is wounded, exhausted or orphaned. There is a human desire to help when confronted with obvious suffering. There are many ways to help but you should not take the decision to care for a bird lightly. Long hours of painstaking feeding and cleaning, as well as round-the-clock attention, are involved. The option of putting an injured bird out of its misery should not be discounted. Remember that the loss of life is naturally so high that neither first aid nor mercy killing will have any effect on the number of birds.

An injured young starling being hand-fed

∴ SURVIVAL AND MORTALITY ∵

T HE LIFE OF A GARDEN bird is short. There are records
of individuals living for many years, but this is unusual.
Although you can do something to increase the likelihood of
wild birds surviving in your garden, nothing can alter the fact
that most birds die young. In general, it is the healthiest birds
that usually manage to survive the vast range of natural
and man made hazards and continue the species.

· LIFE EXPECTANCY ·

It is tempting to think that the robin that
visits your bird-table every winter, or the
swallow nesting in your porch every summer, is the same bird each year. However,
unless they have identifiable features, it is
impossible to be sure that your favourite
birds have not died and been replaced by
lookalikes. Even ornithologists were surprised at the brief life expectancy of small
birds when it was first demonstrated that
about 60% of adult robins die each year
and that three-quarters of young robins
perish before their first birthday.

We are used to the idea that most
people live to a ripe old age so it is hard
to accept that birds suffer heavy losses of

eggs and nestlings. If young birds survive
their hazardous first few weeks, their life
expectancy improves slightly. Even so,
about half to three-quarters of the population of small birds dies each year and the
average life expectancy of an adult song-
bird is only one or two years.

It is also a surprise to learn that mortal-
ity rates may be just as high in summer as
in winter, unless the winter has been particularly severe or the birds have run into
difficulties during migration. We tend to
forget that breeding is a dangerous activity. Males are vulnerable when they are
singing in the open, but females are at a
greater risk because they become sitting
targets on the nest.

As a rule, larger birds live longer than
small ones and longer-lived birds have a
lower breeding rate. If the population is
to remain stable, every pair of birds needs

Double-take *Do not assume that the same
robin* (above) *visits every winter: the odds are
stacked against a bird living for over a year.*

Doomed *A young starling* (right) – *crippled
by a fall from the nest – will die, unless rescued.*

to rear only two offspring to grow up and replace them. When you consider that a pair of blackbirds may lay three or four clutches of three to five eggs in a summer, the countryside would soon be swarming with blackbirds if they all lived. If a brood of ten all survived, simple arithmetic shows that their descendants would number many millions within a decade.

In practice, the breeding population at the end of winter is the same as it was in the previous spring. The lost eggs and young birds are a "doomed surplus" but their short lives are not pointless. They are the raw material that natural selection, the mechanism of evolution, works on. It weeds out the least capable – those that are too slow to notice a prowling cat or too weak to survive a cold night. In the long run only the fittest birds survive to continue their lineage. The surplus also

Winter victim *With seeds hard to find, a bullfinch has succumbed to severe weather. Death comes swiftly if there is not enough food.*

However, not all wild birds die young and a small proportion survive into old age. A tawny owl was found dead 21 years after it had been ringed shortly before it first left the nest. A great tit has survived long enough to reach the grand age of 9 years and 3 months. Other records for longevity (based on studies with ringed birds) include: 29 years for mallard, 21 for swift, 20 for both blackbird and starling, 16 years for kestrel and swallow, 13 for robin and house sparrow, with dunnock reaching 9 and goldcrest, the smallest European bird, managing only 7 years.

Resilient wren *The wren population suffered a sharp drop in the 1960s' freeze-ups, but rapidly recouped its losses.*

enables birds to recover their numbers rapidly after a disaster, such as a hard winter or the failure of an important food crop. The reduced population means that there is more food for the survivors so they breed well and raise more young to restore numbers quickly. Even though the British population of wrens was hit hard by two severe winters in succession (in 1962 and 1963), the survivors managed to increase tenfold over the next decade.

Heat loss *Small birds, like the tiny goldcrest, lose heat quickly, so they are vulnerable in cold weather.*

• CAUSES OF DEATH •

As many as one-third of all eggs fail to hatch. Some are infertile while others have chilled, perhaps because a cold spell has forced the parents to spend too much time off the nest searching for food. Entire clutches are lost when nests are robbed or smashed by torrential rain or high winds.

It is an unpleasant thought that we may contribute to some of these deaths. How often have parent birds scolded us with a barrage of calls while we continue to dig, weed or clip near their nests without realizing what the fuss is all about? The longer the birds are off the nest, the more the eggs become chilled. To make matters worse, inquisitive predators will be attracted to the sound of the disturbance and wait for the returning parent to give away the position of its nest.

To offset the loss of their eggs, a bereaved pair quickly starts a new clutch. They may take two or three attempts to rear a family with the end result that breeding is more successful than egg losses suggest. After hatching, the loss rate drops, if only because the most vulnerable nests have already been lost and birds are less likely to desert nestlings

Egg loss *A duck egg lies broken after it has been partly eaten by a magpie.*

than eggs. Some nestlings die from starvation, by being squashed under the parent or by falling from the nest. Amazingly, young tawny owls are capable of scrambling back up a tree but most other premature leavers, recognizable by their half-grown wings and tail, perish. You can try to put them back (not always easy) or attempt hand-rearing (p.180).

Death by starvation is probably more common in some gardens (if there are no birdfeeders) than in the wild because natural food may be scarce. Over-tidying

Dead redwing *In Scandinavia, the redwing* (above) *nests in gardens but elsewhere it is likely to enter the garden, together with fieldfares, only when food is scarce. It will starve in harsh winters when it is unable to find food.*

Back on top *If a tawny owl nestling* (left) *falls out of its nest before it is fully fledged, it is still able to climb back to it again.*

the garden destroys the rich pickings of insects. Worse, poison sprays aimed at killing insects can harm birds that feed on them. I have faced the dilemma of watching blue tits shuttling between their nestbox and a rosebed where the new buds were crusted with aphids. Spraying the

roses might starve or poison the young tits. The compromise is to choose one of the less toxic insecticides currently available, such as pyrethrum, which is prepared from dried chrysanthemums, or malathion. The traditional treatment with a strong soap solution is also worth a try.

• GARDEN DANGERS •

Compared with these losses from "natural causes", which go largely unnoticed in the garden, the plunderings of nest-robbers, which are distressing to witness, are probably not so serious. It seems that predators are most likely to find nests that are going to fail anyway. When nestlings are starving, their unceasing begging calls alert predators to their presence.

Of all the nest-robbers in the garden, domestic cats are the worst. Rats may also be a problem, together with squirrels and even mice. Jays, crows, jackdaws, rooks and occasionally tawny owls all rob nests regularly but none of them search as systematically as magpies, who will

Rat attack *Rats search for eggs and nestlings; lay bait so the rats can be trapped.*

Chief nest-robber *The nimble skill of the domestic cat, a natural hunter, makes it the chief predator of garden birds.*

Leg of chick

Systematic hunter *It seems likely that magpies mainly steal eggs, and sometimes nestlings, where there is a high density of song-birds, as is the case in gardens.*

despoil an area and then return when their victims have laid replacement clutches. However, it has yet to be proved that magpies have ever caused a dramatic decline in the numbers of garden birds.

Birds nesting in holes, like swifts, tits, jackdaws and sparrows, are obviously safer from predators than those in exposed cup-nests, but nest-boxes are vulnerable to attack from weasels, which are small enough to get in through the entrance. Squirrels can gnaw, and great spotted woodpeckers can chisel through the sides of nest-boxes. Woodpeckers have also learnt the unfortunate trick of reaching in through the entrance hole and pulling the nestlings out.

Once out of the nest, cold and star-vation are the main causes of death but collisions with man-made objects, such as windows and motor vehicles, or rarer accidents, such as becoming tangled in netting or lines of string, also cause fatalities. The live dangers change: cats are still a problem but they are joined by birds of prey. A pair of sparrowhawks and their family need to kill about 2,000 small birds every year. While it is pleasing to know that the garden environment can support such fascinating birds as kestrels, sparrowhawks and owls, and may, exceptionally, attract merlins, peregrines or harriers, one feels a twinge of con-science when birds that we have attracted into an exposed position on a bird-table are swept away by a winged predator.

Woodpecker threat *The great spotted woodpecker* (left) *searches for other birds' nests so it can eat their young. It can even drill through nest-boxes.*

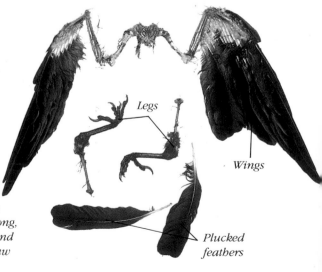

Legs

Wings

Plucked feathers

Surprise attack *You have to be quick to spot the confused flurry of feathers that marks a sparrowhawk attack. The fast-flying sparrowhawk stealthily dashes alongside hedges before pouncing. Its strong, hooked bill* (above) *is used to tear flesh and strip bones bare. The remains of a jackdaw* (right) *show that there is little wasted.*

· REDUCING PREDATION ·

It is not easy to protect birds from predators but there are a few ways to help against persistent attacks. Advocates of aversion therapy keep buckets of water or old potatoes for hurling at cats and magpies. (A direct hit is unnecessary; the shock is sufficient.) A dog should also do the trick, especially if it is let out at dawn when cats and members of the crow family are most active. Collared doves and mistle thrushes are renowned for their

courage in attacking magpies but they cannot be relied upon. Losses of nests are higher early in the breeding season when foliage is still sparse. Dense evergreens consequently provide safer nesting places and clipped hedges produce impenetrable growth that deters cats and magpies. (The disadvantage of trimmed hedges is that they bear smaller crops of berries.)

If a nest looks vulnerable, try protecting it by spreading a nylon mesh over the bush or hedge. This will keep the predators out but let the birds enter underneath. You can also use 5 cm (2 in) wire netting, which small birds can pass through It is best placed in position when the bird has started to incubate. You can protect nest-boxes from cats and other predators by fitting them with a screen of chicken wire. Woodpeckers and squirrels can be kept out by reinforcing the edges of the box with metal strips and by fixing a metal plate (p.111) around the entrance.

Robbed nest A magpie has ripped apart the feather lining (left) of a long-tailed tit's nest.

Look-out An early breeder, the mistle thrush (below) may nest on exposed sites. It will swoop on anyone who comes near its nest.

∴ CARE AND RESCUE ∴

N OT ALL BIRDS THAT look abandoned are orphans and not all ill-looking birds are actually sick. Nevertheless, thousands of birds are discovered in need of help every year. If you find one, the distressing fact may be that the bird needs to be put out of its misery quickly. Remember that if you take a bird into care and nurse it back to health, it may never be able to return to the wild and will need constant supervision. However, if you do have the time and energy for the task, injured birds sometimes respond well to patient care and attention.

• ORPHANS •

The season of "orphan" birds is from mid-April onwards. These are fledglings found hopping across a lawn or sitting quietly under a bush. It is often assumed, especially by children, that these birds have lost their parents and need to be rescued. However, they are only truly orphaned once they have been picked up and carried away. These fledglings look vulnerable and often call plaintively, so it is easy to think that they have been abandoned. In fact, a parent is either in another garden busily looking for food or is waiting in a nearby tree for you to go away. The most common "false orphans" are thrushes, blackbirds and starlings, which tend to leave the nest before they can fly well and struggle to follow their parents while they are collecting food.

Leave these fledglings alone and if one has been "rescued" take it back to where it had been found. It probably has more chance of survival if it is left alone. If you are worried that a young bird is in danger, keep watch from a discreet distance to see if the parents come back, or return in a couple of hours to see how it is doing. If the fledgling is in a particularly exposed place, it should be put on a safe perch, but some fledglings are mobile enough to try escaping and may get into worse trouble if you try to help them.

Some young birds, such as tawny and little owls, leave the nest before they can fly, but others fall out accidentally. The latter can be recognized by their partly formed wing- and tail-feathers. It is dangerous to try to place a bird back in the nest because the others may jump out if disturbed, or some parents may attack. If you put it on a nearby perch, the parents will continue to feed it.

Wait *Despite its air of helplessness, the fledgling song thrush has not been abandoned and a parent will soon come to feed it.*

· CATCHING AND HANDLING ·

Once you decide to help a bird, act firmly. Even a wounded bird can move fast enough to keep out of reach. A one-handed pounce (even if you only catch one wing) does the trick. Use your other hand to stop the bird flapping. Better still, drop a cloth over the bird: this prevents it fluttering and the darkness calms it down.

Once you have caught a small bird, grasp it in one hand, letting its head poke out between your first two fingers. Do not squeeze its body because its heart and lungs are easily squashed. Hold a larger bird in front of you with both your hands around its wings and body. Put a heron or goose under one arm so its wings stay folded, taking care to keep its bill from your face. (You can wrap the bird in a coat to keep its wings in place.)

A firm hold ensures that the bird cannot scratch or peck. Even small birds can draw blood, while the curved bill and talons of a hawk are hard to dislodge from flesh. Wear gloves (p.184) when handling crows or larger birds.

Defence posture *By lying back and presenting its talons, a little owl resists an attempt to pick it up.*

WHAT TO DO WITH A RINGED BIRD

If you find an injured or dead bird with a metal ring, or sometimes one or more plastic ones, on its leg, you can contribute to our understanding of birdlife. Carefully record the number stamped on the ring and, if there are plastic rings, the order of the colours (reading down from "knee" to "ankle"). Look for the address in tiny letters and make a note of it.

Send this information together with your own name and address, the place and date of finding the ring and notes on how you found the bird and the state it was in, to the **British Trust for Ornithology**, Beech Grove, Tring, Hertfordshire. If the bird is dead, remove its ring to send in as well, but do not try to take the ring off a live bird. Eventually you will receive a history of the bird saying where it was ringed. Most birds are found within a few miles of where they were first caught but there is always a chance of finding one with a foreign ring that has come from somewhere exotic.

Birds may be ringed only by people who have undergone a training programme, which qualifies them to hold an official licence. Many of the details of birds' habits in this book have come from studies with ringed birds. This is the only way that researchers can identify individuals. Bird-ringing gave the first proof that our swallows flew to South Africa, and no-one realized just how short the life expectancy of small birds was (p.174) until the results of ringing were analyzed.

Ringed *A dead blackbird has a ring attached to its leg.*

Metal ring

· FIRST AID ·

There is no doubt that most seriously injured birds should be humanely put down to stop their suffering. You should only attempt to care for a badly wounded bird if you are prepared to take it along to the vet for treatment and then accept the responsibility of looking after it during a long convalescence.

If, however, the damage is not too bad, first aid may help. As with a human patient, the first step is to keep a sick or injured bird warm – it will not feed if it is cold. When the bird is looking happier, treat surface cuts and abrasions with a gentian-violet wound spray. Then remove any small, sausage-shaped, pale yellow blowfly eggs, which are laid on animals that are nearly dead. They can be found in the bird's nostrils, ears, mouth and under its tail. Pick them off the skin and feathers with tweezers, and from the nostrils with a wooden cocktail stick.

Invalid *An injured bird, like this tawny owl, is likely to be weak and in a state of shock.*

· HOUSING ·

A rescued bird needs to be kept quiet and warm. Most animals stop struggling when in the dark so will not injure themselves trying to escape. The best place for a sick bird is in a well-ventilated cardboard box with a secure lid. Line the box with newspaper to keep it clean. Better still, use kitchen paper: it is more absorbent and the bird's feet can get a strong grip on the crinkly surface. Keep the box in a warm place, such as an airing cupboard. Make sure it is not too hot: 30°C (86°F) is the maximum temperature.

Do not be surprised if the bird appears to be recovering and then suddenly dies. A bird that is weak enough to let itself be caught is likely to be in a serious condition. Birds brought in by the cat may look only dishevelled but they rarely survive. If the bird does live, make a more permanent home for it. Cover the open front of a wooden box with the same type of wire mesh that is used on the scrap basket (p.99). A perch at each end lets the bird rest in a natural position and prevents it from fouling itself.

· STRIKING WINDOWS ·

As more gardens are equipped with greenhouses, and houses are fitted with picture windows and conservatories, so the toll increases of birds injured and killed by collisions with glass. It seems that the birds either see sky and foliage through the glass, or they mistake reflections for the real thing and are convinced that they are flying towards an open space. Either way, the cure is to stick silhouettes of a hawk (or any pattern you fancy) on to offending panes or to hang some curtains to destroy the reflection.

Sometimes a bird will bounce off the glass and fly to a perch where it can sit and recover. Others drop, stunned, to the ground, where they are easy meat for cats. They may recuperate from their fall quickly but are best kept in a warm, dark place until they become fully active.

· FEEDING ·

Feeding orphans and wounded birds is a messy, time-consuming, but rewarding process. You need great patience for the task because a small bird has to be fed every two hours during the day, and no fewer than four times a day when it grows older. When it is very young, it cannot feed itself at all and you have to act the part of the parents and push food into its mouth. If it is healthy it will open its mouth in a wide gape, allowing you to poke small portions of food down its throat. (If the food is simply dropped into the mouth, the bird may have trouble swallowing it.) A gentle tap on the beak sometimes stimulates a bird to gape. Older birds that have left the nest and are beginning to feed themselves are more difficult to feed. They have become used to their parents and do not gape readily to

Wide gape *A young, orphaned starling receives food from a syringe. A healthy bird will instinctively gape whenever it is hungry.*

Force-fed *Push food down a bird's throat with a pair of tweezers, rather than simply dropping it into its beak. This precaution prevents food blocking the bird's windpipe and choking it.*

a strange foster parent. Gently use your fingernail to prise open the tip of their beaks. With any luck, it will only be a matter of time before the birds learn to gape at the sight of food.

A clean pair of blunt surgical forceps or tweezers can be used to poke food into a bird's mouth, in which case the food needs to be fairly dry. A more effective way of dispensing food is to squirt it into the bird's mouth from a plastic hypodermic syringe (of 1,2,5 or 10 ml size as appropriate) with the tip cut off. You will know when a young bird has had enough of its meal because it will stop gaping.

Jay fledgling

Self-service *After a while your patience will be rewarded as the bird starts to feed itself. Put food for it in plastic pots or glazed dishes that will not easily tip over.*

Kestrel diet An injured
kestrel, the victim of a
collision with a car, is being
fed on thin strips of raw steak
held in bamboo forceps.
This high-protein food
resembles the rodent meat
of its natural diet. Rough-
age, such as fur, should be
added as the bird recovers.

Glove A thick leather
gauntlet gives you the best
protection from the pain-
fully sharp talons and beaks
of owls, hawks and falcons.

strips of meat or grated peanuts according
to the needs of each species. If you have
the time and inclination, collect green caterpillars off foliage or scrape aphids from
unsprayed roses and beans. Alternatively,
you will find it easier simply to cultivate a
colony of mealworms (p.106).

Bread, milk and scrambled egg are not
suitable foods for birds at this stage and
will only cause stomach upsets. Nor is it
a sensible idea to serve birds in your care
with earthworms because they can be
tough and indigestible. Maggots and
caterpillars are acceptable but must be cut
up or they simply pass through the bird's
stomach in one piece. There are, however, few hard-and-fast rules: some
injured birds have been successfully
reared on nothing but catfood.

When the meal is over, remove the baby
bird's faecal sac (droppings encased in a
gelatinous membrane) as the parents
would do. If the bird passes a neat
dropping that you can easily pick up with
a pair of tweezers, you can be fairly sure
that you have got its diet right. If the
dropping is liquid yellow or foul-smelling
brown and you cannot pick it up, then try
a different food or combination of foods.
Think what the parent birds would feed
the baby and try to get as near to that diet
as possible. Once you have identified the
bird, look up its diet, which is indicated in
Bird Profiles (pp.34–89).

The youngest birds can be fed on raw
mince (cut extremely finely) or raw
scraped beef or chicken, mixed with
moist baby cereal. Ground-up vitamin and
mineral (especially calcium) supplements
must be included. As the birds become
older, transfer them to a diet of chick-
crumbs (feed for chicks), grated cheese,
soaked currants, tinned catfood, seeds,

Road to recovery
The neat dropping that this
mallard duckling has
passed indicates that it is
being fed properly.

CARE AND RESCUE

Sick birds, especially, need a high-protein diet, together with foodstuffs that supply instant energy. Give them a mush of very finely scraped beef or chicken (or cat-food) with added minerals and vitamins. Remove uneaten pieces to prevent the spread of diseases. Supplement this diet with water and glucose delivered from a syringe or eyedrop pipette.

Natural food *To start some orphans feeding, it is sometimes necessary to catch wild food for them. Here a fledgling little owl is about to swallow a butterfly.*

· RELEASE ·

Unless they are permanently crippled, birds should not be kept for a moment after they are capable of fending for them-selves. (You will probably be fed up with looking after them by then, anyway!) In natural circumstances, birds such as tits, finches and thrushes do not fly much when they first leave the nest, so let an orphan have some flying practice indoors. Release it only when it is flying strongly and no longer calling to be fed. It is also a sensible idea to check that adult birds that have recovered from fractures or wounds are able to fly properly before they are let loose into the wild.

When the time comes for release, put the bird's wooden box or cage outside so the bird can become accustomed to its surroundings. After a while, open the door. Swallows, martins and swifts should be launched into the air. The release must take place in the morning, in fine weather, so the birds can feed up and find a safe roost before nightfall. (Owls must, of course, be released at night.) Regularly put out food at the release point: some birds, such as tawny owls, crows, tits and blackbirds, will return to feed while they are making the transition to a fully independent existence.

Return visit *If you put out food where you released your bird, it may come back to feed during its first few weeks in the wild. Members of the crow family, like the jackdaw, may return for years.*

Mealworms *A regular supply of mealworms may help tempt many birds to pay another visit.*

∴ CASE HISTORIES ∵

IF YOU ARE PLANNING to look after a wounded or orphaned bird that you have found to be in definite need of help, be prepared for a responsibility that could last as long as the bird itself. Under your care (and free from predators) a bird could live for years – far beyond the ages given for wild birds on page 175, although it may never recover well enough to leave. As a result, you have to take on the guardianship of a bird with as much commitment as taking on a puppy or kitten.

• ORPHAN MOORHEN •

A young moorhen chick was rescued after it had been seen wandering dangerously near to a road, obviously abandoned. When found, it was cold, hungry and frightened. The chick was already several days old and therefore used to its natural parents, which made it difficult to feed. Unlike the young of other ground-dwelling birds, such as pheasants, ducks and domestic fowl, baby moorhens are not instinctively programmed to pick up food for themselves. Instead, they take it from their parents' beaks. As a result, an orphan moorhen has to have food presented in beak-like forceps or tweezers.

To encourage the moorhen chick to be less nervous, some hatchling bantam chicks were put with it. The moorhen huddled with the chicks for company and extra warmth, and their confidence made it much less anxious. The moorhen was now prepared to take food more readily from the forceps. It was soon joining the chicks around the food bowl and cheekily snatching crumbs from their beaks.

Forceps-fed
The baby moorhen (above), *two days after being rescued, would only take food from a pair of beak-mimicking forceps.*

Dinner party
The presence of bantam chicks (left) *helped reassure the moorhen and made it feel more at home in its new surroundings. It was not long before the young bird started to pick up food for itself.*

· CRIPPLED STARLING ·

A starling nestling was in a dreadful state after suffering a long fall from its nest under the eaves of a garage. When the small bird was discovered, it was unable to lift up its head at all, and its left leg stuck out at an unnatural angle to one side. Although the young bird managed to gape well for food, its head had to be held each time it was being fed. For the rest of the time, the young starling either remained curled up in the foetal position, or else spun round helplessly in circles. It was unable to bring itself to adopt the normal crouched position of a nestling.

Day One: Arrival The injured nestling appears brain-damaged because, try as it might, it cannot uncurl its body from the foetal position of a hatchling (p.159).

Day One

Day Six: Housing The starling, now stronger and feathered, was moved to a canary basket, in the hope that, as it could grip the sides with its claws, it might be able to pull itself upright.

Day Six

Day Eight

Day Eight: Improvement After a couple more days, the patient improved to the point where it was able to sit up and perch. Its left leg was still not quite normal and its head was held a little to one side.

Day Ten

Day Ten: Recovery By now the starling could flutter about and toddle, as long as its feet could grip a rough surface, like a towel. Although the bird preferred the comfort of the basket, it could stretch and preen as well as any starling fledgling.

∴ BIRD CLASSIFICATION ∴

The early naturalists devoted much of their time to putting wildlife in order. They gave plants and animals scientific names and classified them according to their relationships with one another.

When you start observing the birds in your garden, it is not always easy to sort out the different kinds. There seem to be so many small, brown birds – how are they related to each other? A greenfinch is very like a chaffinch, but are the finches close relatives of the similar-looking house sparrows? Ducks, geese and swans are clearly similar in appearance and behaviour but what about the relationship between jays, magpies and crows, or swallows, swifts and martins?

Zoologists and botanists use a system to name and classify animals and plants that shows the connections between them. It was devised by Carolus Linnaeus over 200 years ago. He gave all living things a two-word scientific name in Latin or ancient Greek – international languages. The first word always states the genus; the second word is the species name. For example, *Passer* is the Latin for sparrow: the house sparrow is called *Passer domesticus* and the tree sparrow *Passer montanus*. Sharing the same genus name means that the two species have similarities. However, the scientific name for dunnock is *Prunella modularis*. This shows that the dunnock is not closely related to the sparrows, and explains why its old name of hedge sparrow is inaccurate.

Linnaeus also grouped every genus with strong points of resemblance into families, and classified the families with broadly similar characteristics into orders. For instance, fieldfares, robins, blackbirds, and thrushes belong to the family *Turdidae*. Swallows and martins are grouped in the family *Hirundinidae* but swifts are in the *Apodidae* family, although they have a similar lifestyle. The *Turdidae* and *Hirundinidae* families, together with others such as the finch family (*Fringillidae*), are all in the order *Passeriformes* (the sparrow-like birds), which includes all the perching birds and songbirds. Swifts, with their different, four, forward-pointing toes, belong to the order *Apodiformes*, which contains the most aerial of birds.

The table of species opposite shows the relationships between birds illustrated in this book. You can learn some interesting things from this bird classification. For example, you can see that long-tailed tits are not related to other tits and that barn owls are rather different from other owls.

Carolus Linnaeus *The Swedish naturalist, Carolus Linnaeus, originated the classification system in his* Systema Naturae *of 1758.*

• BIRDS IN THEIR FAMILIES AND ORDERS •

ORDER	FAMILY	COMMON AND SCIENTIFIC NAMES
Pelecaniformes	*Phalacrocoracidae*	Cormorant *(Phalacrocorax carbo)*
Ciconiiformes	*Ardeidae*	Grey heron *(Ardea cinerea)*
Anseriformes	*Anatidae*	Mallard *(Anas platyrhynchos)*
Accipitriformes	*Accipitridae*	Sparrowhawk *(Accipiter nisus)*
Falconiformes	*Falconidae*	Kestrel *(Falco tinnunculus)*
Galliformes	*Phasianidae*	Pheasant *(Phasianus colchicus)*
Gruiformes	*Rallidae*	Moorhen *(Gallinula chloropus)*, Coot *(Fulica atra)*.
Charadriiformes	*Laridae*	Black-headed gull *(Larus ridibundus)*, Herring gull *(Larus argentatus)*, Lesser black-backed gull *(Larus fuscus)*.
Columbiformes	*Columbidae*	Collared dove *(Streptopelia decaocto)*, Street pigeon *(Columba livia)*, Woodpigeon *(Columba palumbus)*.
Psittaciformes	*Psittacidae*	Budgerigar *(Melopsittacus undulatus)*
Cuculiformes	*Cuculidae*	Cuckoo *(Cuculus canorus)*
Strigiformes	*Tytonidae*	Barn owl *(Tyto alba)*
	Strigidae	Tawny owl *(Strix aluco)*, Little owl *(Athene noctua)*.
Apodiformes	*Apodidae*	Swift *(Apus apus)*
Coraciiformes	*Alcedinidae*	Kingfisher *(Alcedo atthis)*
Piciformes	*Picidae*	Green woodpecker *(Picus viridis)*, Great spotted woodpecker *(Dendrocopos major)*.
Passeriformes	*Hirundinidae*	House martin *(Delichon urbica)*, Swallow *(Hirundo rustica)*.
	Motacillidae	Pied wagtail *(Motacilla alba)*, Meadow pipit *(Anthus pratensis)*.
	Troglodytidae	Wren *(Troglodytes troglodytes)*
	Prunellidae	Dunnock *(Prunella modularis)*
	Sylviidae	Goldcrest *(Regulus regulus)*, Willow warbler *(Phylloscopus trochilus)*, Chiffchaff *(Phylloscopus collybita)*.
	Muscicapidae	Spotted flycatcher *(Muscicapa striata)*
	Turdidae	Fieldfare *(Turdus pilaris)*, Robin *(Erithacus rubecula)*, Blackbird *(Turdus merula)*, Song thrush *(Turdus philomelos)*, Mistle thrush *(Turdus viscivorus)*, Redwing *(Turdus iliacus)*, Black redstart *(Phoenicurus ochruros)*, Nightingale *(Luscinia megarhynchos)*.
	Aegithalidae	Long-tailed tit *(Aegithalos caudatus)*
	Paridae	Blue tit *(Parus caeruleus)*, Great tit *(Parus major)*, Coal tit *(Parus ater)*, Marsh tit *(Parus palustris)*.
	Sittidae	Nuthatch *(Sitta europaea)*
	Certhiidae	Treecreeper *(Certhia familiaris)*
	Emberizidae	Reed bunting *(Emberiza schoeniclus)*
	Fringillidae	Chaffinch *(Fringilla coelebs)*, Goldfinch *(Carduelis carduelis)*, Greenfinch *(Carduelis chloris)*, Siskin *(Carduelis spinus)*, Bullfinch *(Pyrrhula pyrrhula)*, Crossbill *(Loxia curvirostra)*.
	Passeridae	House sparrow *(Passer domesticus)*
	Sturnidae	Starling *(Sturnus vulgaris)*
	Corvidae	Jay *(Garrulus glandarius)*, Magpie *(Pica pica)*, Carrion crow *(Corvus corone)*, Rook *(Corvus frugilegus)*, Jackdaw *(Corvus monedula)*.

∴ INDEX ∴

· ACKNOWLEDGMENTS ·

Author's acknowledgments
I would like to thank Jane Burton for contributing her
expert knowledge on the care of sick and wounded birds.
She supplied invaluable material and, most helpfully, the
photography and text for the case studies. Many thanks are
also due to David Lamb for a guiding hand and to the staff
of the RSPB, especially Ian Dawson, for advice and
assistance during the preparation of the book.

Photographer's acknowledgments
Many thanks to Jane Burton for her help and encourage-
ment throughout the production of the book. She took a lot
of photographs especially for the book and provided many
others from her library. I would also like to thank Gary
Huggins for his enthusiasm and hard work in tracking down
and photographing some of the more elusive birds. A
number of people either loaned tame birds or helped me
find places where birds could be photographed. I would
particularly like to thank Yvette Cameron, Margaret Cawsey,
Peggy and Tony Davies, Derek and Jill Mills, Malcolm Sharp,
Mike Smith, Mrs. E.G. Taylor, Jenny Tyson-Jones, and
Carolyn and Michael Woods.

Dorling Kindersley would like to thank the following
people for their help during the preparation of this book:
Hilary Bird for the index; Ian Bishop and Michael Walters
of the Zoological Museum, Tring for research on nests; Liza
Bruml, Josephine Buchanan and Andrew Mikolajski for
editorial assistance; Jane Burton, Tony Graham and John
Woodcock for illustrations; Bruce Coleman Limited for
photographs; Nick Harris for DTP expertise; Peter Luff for
jacket design; Maryann Rogers and Teresa Solomon for
production; and Mustafa Sami for building the feeders and
nest-boxes. Also, special thanks to Debra Royal at the RSPB.

All photographs taken by **Kim Taylor** especially for the
RSPB Birdfeeder Handbook apart from the following
contributions:

James Baldwin 171t **Jane Burton** 28t; 37b; 41br; 42cr, b;
43cl; 48t, c; 49t; 50cl, cr; 65cl; 92l; 93cr; 151tl, tr; 164; 172;
174r; 177cl, cr; 181t; 183t, c, b; 184t, b; 185t; 186–7; 192
Robert Burton 8t; 19t, b; 20c, br; 22t; 27bl; 73br; 109b; 119l,
r; 120t; 137cr; 138r; 167tl; 170b; 176br **Peter Chadwick** 7;
14cl, c, br; 20tr; 31; 33b; 41c; 43cr; 45c; 47c; 56br; 59b; 67c;
69cr; 71cr; 86c; 91; 152bl; 156bc, br; 157c, b; 171c **John
Daniels** 67t **Geoff Dann** 20bl; 81tr **Philip Dowell** 39br;
89c **Gary Huggins** 24tl; 25tl, tr; 29tr; 48b; 50b; 53b; 121b;
160br; 166t; 167tr; 176bl **Jacqui Hurst** 170c **Colin Keates**
154–5 **David Lamb** 12r **Royal Horticultural Society
(Lindley Library)** 188

Courtesy of Bruce Coleman Limited:
Jane Burton 10tr; 24b; 30; 34b; 37cl, b; 38b; 40b; 43b; 45cr;
47b; 56bl; 57cl; 61b; 74t; 75b; 76b; 79b; 84b; 88b; 89b;
120br; 133cl; 134; 136b; 137bl; 153b; 158tr; 159t, c, b; 160l;
162b; 163c; 169b; 175t; 180; 182 **Kim Taylor** 9b; 13b; 20tl;
33t; 36br; 51cl; 53t; 55tr, br; 58t, b; 59t; 61t; 62c; 63b; 64l;
65cr, b; 66cr; 67b; 68br; 69cl, b; 70b; 71b; 72b; 73cr; 74b;
77b; 82cr; 83t, c, b; 90; 93b; 108br; 116; 118b; 121t; 122l;
124b; 125t; 126t; 128; 129t, c, bl, br; 135c, b; 136c; 142r;
143t; 144b; 148t, br; 153t; 157t; 161b; 162t, c; 163t, b; 166r;
168l; 171b; 178bl **Hans Reinhard** 28b **Roger
Wilmshurst** 82b

Abbreviations: b=bottom, c=centre, l=left, r=right, t=top.

The Royal Society for the Protection of Birds is *the*
charity that takes action for wild birds and the environment.
Supported by over half a million subscribing members, the
RSPB is Europe's largest wildlife conservation body.